Fodor's

# MUNICH'S
# 25 BEST

**WITH FULL-SIZE FOLDOUT MAP**

# Munich Map

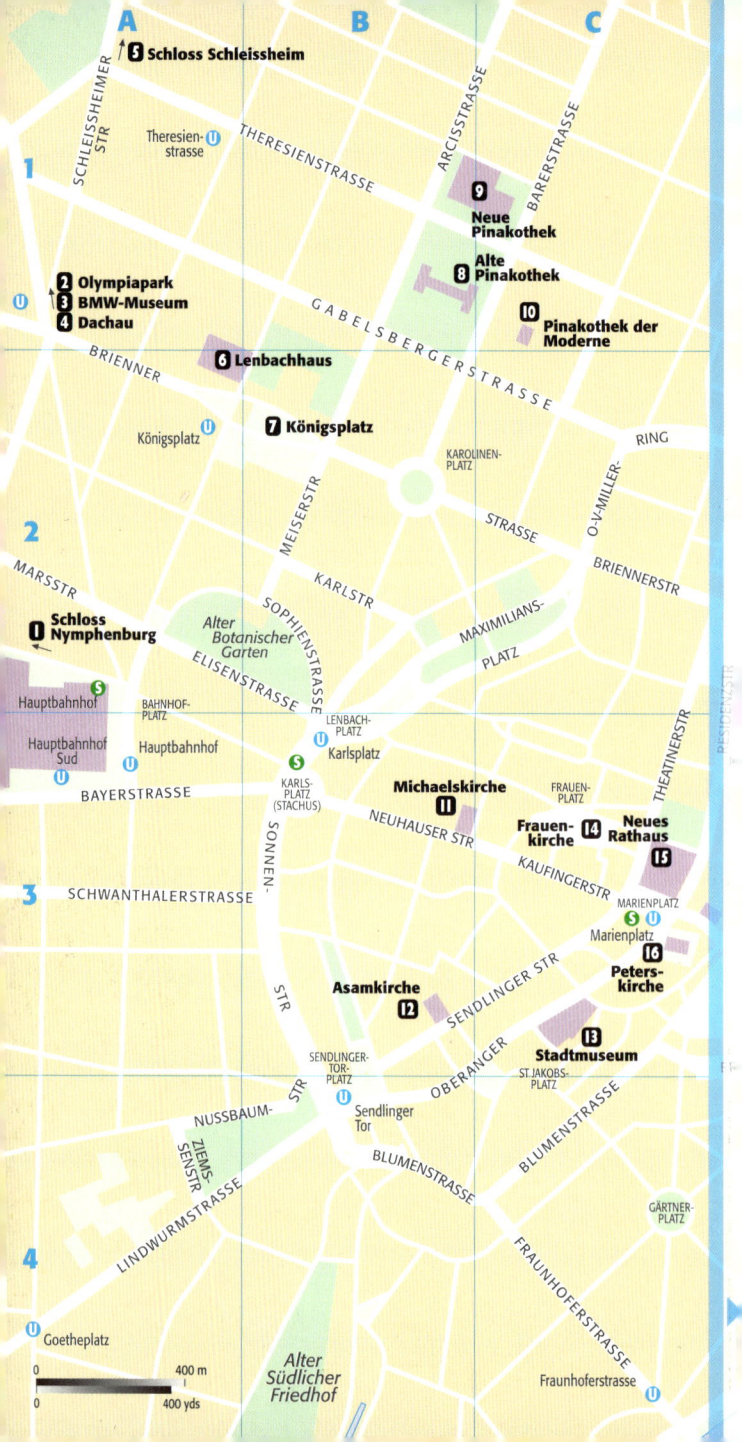

## Grid A
- **Schloss Schleissheim**
- **2** Olympiapark
- **3** BMW-Museum
- **4** Dachau
- **1** Schloss Nymphenburg

## Grid B
- **6** Lenbachhaus
- **7** Königsplatz
- **11** Michaelskirche
- **12** Asamkirche
- **13** Stadtmuseum

## Grid C
- **9** Neue Pinakothek
- **8** Alte Pinakothek
- **10** Pinakothek der Moderne
- **14** Frauenkirche
- **15** Neues Rathaus
- **16** Peterskirche

## Streets and Places
- SCHLEISSHEIMER STR
- Theresienstrasse
- THERESIENSTRASSE
- ARCISSTRASSE
- BARERSTRASSE
- GABELSBERGERSTRASSE
- BRIENNER
- Königsplatz
- MEISERSTR
- KAROLINENPLATZ
- O-V-MILLER-STRASSE
- RING
- BRIENNERSTR
- MARSSTR
- KARLSTR
- SOPHIENSTRASSE
- MAXIMILIANSPLATZ
- Alter Botanischer Garten
- ELISENSTRASSE
- Hauptbahnhof
- BAHNHOFPLATZ
- Hauptbahnhof Sud
- Hauptbahnhof
- BAYERSTRASSE
- LENBACHPLATZ
- Karlsplatz
- KARLSPLATZ (STACHUS)
- NEUHAUSER STR
- FRAUENPLATZ
- THEATINERSTR
- KAUFINGERSTR
- SONNENSTR
- SCHWANTHALERSTRASSE
- MARIENPLATZ
- Marienplatz
- SENDLINGER STR
- OBERANGER
- ST JAKOBSPLATZ
- SENDLINGER-TOR-PLATZ
- Sendlinger Tor
- NUSSBAUMSTR
- ZIEMSSENSTR
- BLUMENSTRASSE
- LINDWURMSTRASSE
- FRAUNHOFERSTRASSE
- GÄRTNERPLATZ
- Goetheplatz
- Alter Südlicher Friedhof
- Fraunhoferstrasse

0 400 m
0 400 yds

Top 25 locator map
(continues on inside
back cover)

# Fodor's
# MUNICH'S 25 BEST

by Teresa Fisher

Fodor's Travel Publications
New York • Toronto •
London • Sydney • Auckland
www.fodors.com

# About This Book

## KEY TO SYMBOLS

🗺 Map reference to the accompanying fold-out map and Top 25 locator map

✉ Address

☎ Telephone number

🕐 Opening/closing times

🍴 Restaurant or café on premises or nearby

🚆 Nearest railway station

Ⓢ Nearest subway (tube) station

🚌 Nearest bus route

⛴ Nearest riverboat or ferry stop

♿ Facilities for visitors with disabilities

✋ Admission charges: Expensive (over €5), Moderate (€3–€5) and Inexpensive (under €3 )

↔ Other nearby places of interest

❓ Other practical information

▶ Indicates the page where you will find a fuller description

ℹ Tourist information

## ORGANIZATION

This guide is divided into six sections:
- Planning Ahead, Getting There
- Living Munich—Munich Now, Munich Then, Time to Shop, Out and About, Walks, Munich by Night
- Munich's Top 25 Sights
- Munich's Best—best of the rest
- Where To—detailed listings of restaurants, hotels, shops and nightlife
- Travel Facts—practical information

In addition, easy-to-read side panels provide extra facts and snippets, highlights of places to visit and invaluable practical advice.

The colours of the tabs on the page corners match the colours of the triangles aligned with the chapter names on the contents page opposite.

## MAPS

**The fold-out map** in the wallet at the back of this book is a comprehensive street plan of Munich. The first (or only) grid reference given for each attraction refers to this map. **The Top 25 locator map** found on the inside front and back covers of the book itself is for quick reference. It shows the Top 25 Sights, described on pages 26–50, which are clearly plotted by number (**1**–**25**, not page number) across the city. The second map reference given for the Top 25 Sights refers to this map.

# Contents

**PLANNING AHEAD, GETTING THERE**    4 – 7

**LIVING MUNICH**    8 – 24

**MUNICH'S TOP 25 SIGHTS**    25 – 50

1. Schloss Nymphenburg *26*
2. Olympiapark *27*
3. BMW-Museum *28*
4. Dachau *29*
5. Schleissheim Palaces *30*
6. Lenbachhaus (City Gallery) *31*
7. Königsplatz *32*
8. Alte Pinakothek (Old Picture Gallery) *33*
9. Neue Pinakothek (New Picture Gallery) *34*
10. Pinakothek der Moderne *35*
11. Michaelskirche *36*
12. Asamkirche *37*
13. Münchner Stadtmuseum (Munich City Museum) *38*
14. Frauenkirche *39*
15. Neues Rathaus (New Town Hall) *40*
16. Peterskirche *41*
17. Spielzeugmuseum (Toy Museum) *42*
18. Viktualienmarkt *43*
19. Odeonplatz *44*
20. Residenz *45*
21. Hofbräuhaus *46*
22. Nationaltheater *47*
23. Deutsches Museum *48*
24. Englischer Garten *49*
25. Bayerisches Nationalmuseum (Bavarian National Museum) *50*

**MUNICH'S BEST**    51 – 62

**WHERE TO**    63 – 88

**TRAVEL FACTS**    89 – 93

**INDEX**    94 – 95

**CREDITS AND ACKNOWLEDGMENTS**    96

# Planning Ahead

## WHEN TO GO

Munich is busiest between April and September when the weather is at its best. May is the start of the beer garden season while, in summer, the city is popular for its opera festival and lively park life. Autumn draws beer-lovers to the *Oktoberfest* (► 54) and December is crowded with Christmas shoppers here for the Christmas market.

## TIME

Munich is one hour ahead of the UK, six hours ahead of New York and nine hours ahead of Los Angeles.

## AVERAGE DAILY MAXIMUM TEMPERATURES

| JAN | FEB | MAR | APR | MAY | JUN | JUL | AUG | SEP | OCT | NOV | DEC |
|-----|-----|-----|-----|-----|-----|-----|-----|-----|-----|-----|-----|
| 34°F | 34°F | 46°F | 57°F | 64°F | 69°F | 76°F | 74°F | 67°F | 57°F | 44°F | 38°F |
| 1°C | 1°C | 8°C | 14°C | 18°C | 21°C | 24°C | 23°C | 19°C | 14°C | 7°C | 3°C |

**Spring** (March to May) is at its most delightful in May, with mild days and the least rainfall.
**Summer** (June to August) is the sunniest season, with blue skies and long, hazy days, but also the occasional thunderstorms.
**Autumn** (September to November) is often still warm and sunny—so called *Altweibersommer* ('old wives summer').
**Winter** (December to February) is the coldest time of year, with frequent snowfalls.

## WHAT'S ON

**February** *Fasching*: Highpoint of the carnival season, which begins in Nov (► 54).
**March** *Starkbierzeit*: Strong beer season (► 54).
**April** *Spring Festival*: A two-week mini *Oktoberfest* at the Theresienwiese.
*Ballet Festival Week*.
*Auer Mai Dult*: First of three annual fairs and flea markets.
**May** *May Day* (1 May): Traditional maypole dancing at the Viktualienmarkt.
*Maibockzeit*: A season of special strong lagers originating from North Germany.
*Corpus Christi* (second Thu after Whitsun): A magnificent Catholic procession dating back to 1343.
**June** *Spargelzeit*: Celebrates the many ways there are to serve asparagus.
*Founding of Munich* (14 Jun): From Marienplatz to Odeonsplatz the streets fill with music, street theatre and refreshment stalls.
*Film Festival*: A week of international cinematic art.
*Tollwood Festival*: The Olympiapark hosts an alternative festival of rock, jazz, cabaret, food and folklore.
**July** *Opera Festival*: The climax of the cultural year.
*Jacobi Dult*: The second annual Dult.
*Kocherlball*: A traditional workers' ball at 6am in the English Garden.
**August** *Summer Festival*: Two weeks of fireworks and festivities in Olympiapark.
**September** *Oktoberfest* (► 54): The world's largest beer festival.
**October** *Kirchweih Dult*: the third annual Dult.
*German Art and Antiques Fair*.
**December** *Christkindlmarkt* (► 54): Christmas market.

## MUNICH ONLINE

**www.muenchen-tourist.de**
The official Munich Tourist Office website, which is updated regularly, including on-line hotel reservations and general information on the local weather, city sights, guided tours, shopping, restaurants, nightlife and special events.

**www.munichfound.de**
Website for the monthly English-language magazine *Munich Found*, catering to visitors and residents alike containing tips on local events, a comprehensive city guide and restaurant and entertainment listings, as well as sports and activities for children.

**www.munich-partyguide.de**
Up-to-date information on Munich's nightlife scene with details of all the latest bars and clubs. A must for party animals.

**www.schloesser.bayern.de**
A comprehensive and informative guide to palaces, castles, fortresses, residences, parks, gardens and lakes in Munich and throughout Bavaria.

**www.museen-in-bayern.de**
Detailed site covering 50 museums in Munich alone, as well as in the surrounding region.

**www.travelforkids.com/funtodo/Germany/munich.htm**
Brief descriptions of attractions for children and families in and around Munich.

**www.mvv-muenchen.de/en**
Everything you could wish to know about the Munich transport system, with maps, electronic timetables, tickets and prices for the city's *S-Bahn* (urban rail), *U-Bahn* (underground), trams and buses.

**www.biergarten.com**
A comprehensive guide (in German only) to the best of Munich's beer gardens.

## GOOD TRAVEL SITES

**www.munich-airport.de**
For details of flight arrivals and departures, general travel information, airport facilities and transport links with the city.

**www.fodors.com**
A complete travel planning site. You can research prices and weather; book air tickets, cars and rooms; pose questions to fellow travellers and find links to other useful sites.

## CYBERCAFÉS

**Cyberice**
O23 Sendlinger-tor-Platz 5 18 91 22 20 Daily 10am–1am 50c for 5 minutes; €5 an hour

**Internet Point**
N24 Marienplatz 20 (underground) 20 70 27 37 24 hours €1 for 30 minutes; €2 an hour

**Palmis Net Tuner Lounge**
L24 Occamstrasse 9 18 91 33 50 Tue–Sun noon–11pm €1 for 15 minutes

# Getting There

**ENTRY REQUIREMENTS**

EU nationals need a passport or national identity card. Citizens of the US, Canada, Australia and New Zealand need a passport to stay for up to three months. Make sure you have at least six months remaining on your passport.

**MONEY**

The euro (€) is the official currency of Germany. Notes in denominations of 5, 10, 20, 50, 100, 200, and 500 euros, and coins in denominations of 1, 2, 5, 10, 20, and 50 cents, and 1 and 2 euros, were introduced in 2002.

€10

€50

€200

€500

**ARRIVING**

Munich's international airport, Flughafen München Franz-Josef-Strauss, is located 28km (17.5 miles) north of the city, and offers services to over 150 destinations world-wide. Facilities include a bank, pharmacy and a medical centre, as well as a variety of shops, restaurants and cafés.

### ARRIVING AT FLUGHAFEN MÜNCHEN FRANZ-JOSEF-STRAUSS

For 24-hour flight information ☎ 97 52 13 13. The S-Bahn (urban train network) offers two services to the city's hub from platfoms located beneath the airport's main shopping area. S-Bahn 8 runs every 20 minutes from 4.05am until 1.05am, while S-Bahn 1 runs every 20 minutes from 5.55am until 12.15am, and also Monday to Friday at 4.35am and weekends at 5.35am. Buy tickets from the machines in the shopping area before going down to the platform. Remember to stamp your ticket in the blue punching-machine (*Entwerter*) on the platform to validate it before boarding the train. A single journey to the heart of the city costs €8.40. Alternatively, an airport bus leaves Munich North Terminal every 20 minutes from 6.20am–9.40pm, taking 45 minutes to reach the main railway station. A single ticket costs €9.50.

### ARRIVING BY BUS

There are frequent coach links with other German cities, starting from the main bus terminal beside the main railway station.

## ARRIVING BY TRAIN
Trains take around 18 hours to Munich from Calais, in France, or Ostend, in Belgium. Munich has good connections with most major European cities. Most trains terminate at the main station (Hauptbahnhof). The east station (Ostbahnhof) takes regular motorail services from other German stations and from Paris, Budapest, Athens, Istanbul and Rimini. Train information from the German National Railway (Deutsche Bahn) is available in the main station's Travel Centre (Reisezentrum) ☎ 1 18 61.

## ARRIVING BY CAR
Munich is well served by motorways and a ring road provides easy access to the middle of the city. Follow the clearly marked speed restrictions. Fines are harsh. Street parking is difficult in the city centre. Car parks charge around €16 a day. Try the Parkhaus am Stachus (Adolf-Kolping-Strasse 10) or the Parkgarage an der Opera (Max-Joseph-Platz 4).

## GETTING AROUND
U-Bahn (underground) and S-Bahn (suburban trains) provide a regular service within 40km (25 miles) of central Munich. Routes are referred to by their final stop. Underground trains run every five or 10 minutes from about 5am–1am. Tickets are available from automatic ticket machines at stations, MVV sales points in many stations, or in newspaper shops. Before boarding a train, you must put your ticket in the blue punching machine (*Entwerter*).

On buses and trams you must stamp your ticket upon boarding. Single tickets can be bought from the driver (with small change only). Multiple tickets, also valid for U- and S-Bahn, can be bought from vending machines at train stations, but not from the driver. Some trams have ticket vending machines on board. Bus and tram routes are numbered and the vehicle has a destination board showing where it is going to. Seven late-night bus lines and four tram lines operate between the heart of the city and the suburbs once an hour from 1am–4am. For more information on travel ➤ 90–91.

## INSURANCE
Check your policy and buy any necessary supplements. EU nationals receive free emergency medical treatment with the relevant documentation (form E111 for Britons) but full travel insurance is still advised and is vital for all other travellers.

## VISITORS WITH DISABILITIES
Access for visitors with disabilities is generally good in Munich, although some older attractions and churches have few facilities. The Tourist Office's brochure *Munich for Physically Challenged Tourists* contains useful information on travel, lodgings, restaurants, arts and culture, city tours and leisure, and the MVV publishes a map detailing transport facilities. For more information contact the Städtischer Beraterkreis Behinderte Geschäftsstelle (central advice bureau for people with disabilities) ✉ Burgstrasse 4 ☎ 23 32 11 78 or 23 32 11 79.

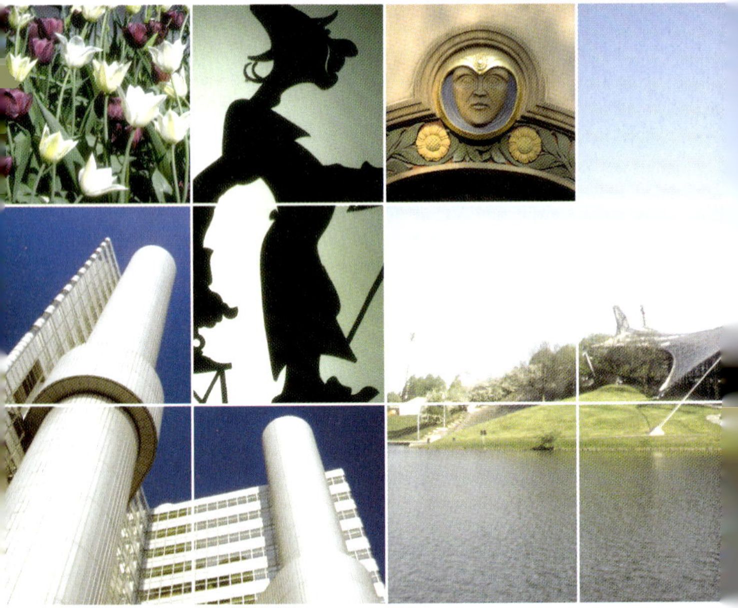

# Living
# Munich

Munich Now *10–15*

Munich Then *16–17*

Time to Shop *18–19*

Out and About *20–21*

Walks *22–23*

Munich by Night *24*

# Munich Now

*Above: Detail of the powerful modern sculpture in front of Alte Pinakothek*

'What is Munich all about? Royal palaces? An artists's city? Bolshevism? Or white sausages?' The question once posed by artist Kurt Schwitters apparently has no answer. Yet surveys show it is Germany's most popular city and that, given the choice, over half the German population would choose to live in Munich, the capital of Bavaria. Those who do live here claim it is more than just an exceptionally attractive city. It radiates a unique atmosphere hard to define although many have tried: 'village of a million',

## DISTRICTS

- The geographical and social core of Munich is the Alstadt (old town), centred on Marienplatz with its neo-Gothic Rathaus (town hall). To the south, beyond the traditional, open-air Viktualienmarkt (food market), the Gärtnerplatz quarter offers some of the city's trendiest bars and nightspots. The commercial core is focused around the designer boutiques of Maximilianstrasse, near the operahouse. Northeast is the English Garden, one of Europe's largest city parks. Bordering it to the west is Schwabing, a vibrant district of fashion shops, bars and restaurants, and also the university quarter. Further west, the Kunstareal (art district) boasts a dazzling selection of museums, including the three celebrated Pinakothek art galleries, the Glyptothek (Sculpture Museum) and the Antikensammlungen (State Collections of Antiquities), enabling visitors to experience two millennia of occidental art.

# Living **Munich**

## GREEN MUNICH

- One of the main reasons for Munich's popularity is its wonderful situation, less than an hour to the Alps and a stone's throw from Austria, Italy and Switzerland. At the weekends, there is a mass exodus to the villages, lakes and mountains for a host of sporting activities, whatever the season.

Left: *Strolling and cycling in the shade of the mature trees lin the English Garden close to the middle of Munich*
Below left: *The broad steps in front of the Neue Pinakothek (New Picture Gallery)*

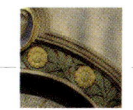

metropolis with a heart', 'Athens on the Isar', 'village of palaces', even 'the secret capital of Germany'. The list of ornamental epithets goes on…

To understand Munich, you really need to understand the Bavarian people. It is their smug patriotism and deep-rooted conservatism that underpins the city, creating a rare balance of German urban efficiency and rural alpine romanticism. The clichéd image many have of a 'typical' German man is actually a Bavarian, sporting leather shorts, feasting on sausage and dumplings, and accompanied by a busty *Dirndl*-clad lady carrying at least a dozen huge *Steins* of beer (27 is the current record). For here, *Lederhosen* and felt hats with tufts resembling shaving brushes are *de rigeur*—part of a cherished folk tradition—and an outward proclamation of proud Bavarian individuality. Don't worry if you can't understand the dialect—most Germans have the same problem.

## Munich Now

Above: *Sculpture featuring a fountain in the Botanischer Garten*
Above right: *Munich's ultra-modern airport*

### A MYSTERY WIND

- The famous *Föhn* wind, Munich's unique weather phenomenon, can strike at any time of year. This warm, dry Alpine wind guarantees blue skies and crystal-clear views (the Alps seem close enough to touch) but it is also blamed for headaches and bad moods. So if barmaids seem more short-tempered and the locals blunter than usual, perhaps it's the *Föhn*!

Native born Münchners are a rarity. The majority of inhabitants come from other parts of Germany, although they all regard themselves as Munich citizens in spirit. Nearly a quarter of the population is foreign, giving Munich a truly international flavour. The city's social scene is fast and fun, with a thriving student population crammed into the bars and cafés of trendy Schwabing, but it is in the old town around Marienplatz where the city's heart beats loudest. Munich is a city of writers, artists, musicians and film-makers, the rich and the jet-set, who cruise the boulevards in their Porsche convertibles.

Take the U-Bahn (underground) at 6am and you will find a lot of sleepy-looking people going to work. They are your average Münchners: diligent, efficient, dedicated to their work but even more dedicated to their *Freizeit* (free time). Perhaps it is the close proximity to Italy which causes lunch hours to get longer and the working day to get shorter? Come 3 o'clock many are back on the tube, and heading for the city's legendary beer gardens, as the Münchners' real joy is to drink a cool beer in the shade of

Living **Munich**

*Student house in Munich's Olympic Village*

chestnut trees in the English Garden. The jovial atmosphere of the beer gardens, where social distinctions cease to matter, brings out the best in everyone: the Bavarian *joie de vivre*, a passion for outdoor life, sociability and an infectious determination to enjoy. Don't be surprised if a stranger links arms with you to sway to the music of an oom-pah band.

Beer plays an unashamedly important role in city life, with Munich acknowledged internationally as the top beer metropolis, and its *Oktoberfest* a household term all over the

### MUNICH & NAZISM

● Munich will always be associated with Adolf Hitler. Indeed he once remarked 'Munich is the city closest to my heart. Here as a young man, as a soldier and as a politician I made my start'. It was here, at the famous bloody Bear Hall Putsch of 1923 when he stormed a meeting of local dignitaries in the Bürgerbräukeller, that he made his first bid for power, launching his career as leader of the Nazi party and giving the world a taste of events to come.

### MANN'S SHINING CITY

● '*München Leuchtet*' ('Munich shone'), the opening words of *Gladius Dei* (1902) by the celebrated German writer and Nobel Prize winner, Thomas Mann, is without doubt one of Munich's most famous quotations. Today, Munich remains Mann's shining city. His words are on its medal of honour—'Munich shines—on Munich's friends'.

# Munich Now

Above: *Crowded tables in the light and beautifully decorated beer tent during Munich's 16-day-long Oktoberfest*
Above right: *An arcade bordering the Hofgarten*

world. Where else in the world is drinking considered the main activity for weeks at a stretch, and its beer festivals counted as 'seasons'? Munich's breweries play a significant economic role, alongside a thriving service industry. After Frankfurt, Munich is Germany's largest banking centre, headquarters of the country's insurance sector and a leading centre of fashion and film-making. It is a huge publishing and media city, second only to New York, and a major national industrial city, with names like Siemens, BMW and Deutsche Aerospace at the heart of its future-orientated vision. However, Munich also has the unenviable reputation as Germany's most expensive city, with spiralling rents and expensive public

## MÜNCHNERS

- 'People are so kind to us that we feel already quite at home, sip baierisch Bier with great tolerance, and talk bad German with more and more aplomb' (George Eliot, 1858).
- 'When I got to know the people of Munich, who at first had seemed somewhat dull and blunt, then I learned to respect both the city and the people. They are hospitable, charming, artistic, colourful and happy' (Felix Philippi, 1870).

Living **Munich**

transport making the cost of living beyond the reach of many people.

We cannot ignore the Bavarian capital's close associations with the rise of Nazism. However we can be grateful that after World War II, although half its buildings were reduced to rubble, unlike so many German cities it chose to restore and reconstruct the great palaces and churches of its past, re-creating one of Europe's most beautiful cities with its historic buildings, handsome parks and world-class museums, galleries and theatres.

So what *is* Munich all about? A village of a million or a bustling metropolis? A big city atmosphere with rural charm? A mixture of central European efficiency and Mediterranean '*savoir vivre*', of BMW and the bohemian, of technology and tradition or just a *gemütlich*, good-time city? There's no denying, this special 'Munich mix' has helped the capital of Bavaria to achieve world renown. As Ernest Hemingway remarked in 1923, 'don't bother going anywhere else…nothing can match Munich. Everything else in Germany is a waste of time'.

*Exhibits in the Glyptothek or Sculpture Museum which houses Greek and Roman sculpture*

### VITAL STATISTICS

- Münchners are the world's largest consumers of beer, downing an annual 190L (42 gal) per head.

- Munich has six main breweries, and produces 5.8 million hectolitres (3.5 million barrels) of beer each year.

- Munich has Germany's largest university, with over 84,000 students.

- Munich has 25,000 bicycle owners.

# Munich Then

Above: *A detail of a ceiling of the Schloss Linderhof, built for Ludwig II*
Above right: *Detail of a tapestry inspired by Wagner's music, decorating the Singers' Hall within Schloss Neuschwanstei*

**LUDWIG I, II & III**

Between 1825 and 1848 King Ludwig I transformed Munich into the Athens on the Isar, a flourishing centre of art and learning, and a university city. In 1848 the king abdicated following political unrest and an affair with dancer Lola Montez.
In 1886 Ludwig II was certified insane and later found mysteriously drowned in Lake Starnberg.
King Ludwig III was deposed in 1918 in the Bavarian Revolution, led by Kurt Eisner, Bavaria's first Prime Minister.

**777** First recorded mention of *Munichen* ('the home of the monks').

**1158** Henry the Lion founds Munich.

**1327** Munich suffers a devastating fire.

**1328** Ludwig IV is made Holy Roman Emperor and Munich becomes temporarily the imperial capital.

**1505** Munich becomes the capital of Bavaria.

**1634** The plague reduces Munich's population by one third, to 9,000.

**1806** Bavaria becomes a kingdom.

**1810** A horse race celebrating the marriage of Crown Prince Ludwig starts the tradition of the *Oktoberfest*.

**1864** Composer Richard Wagner moves to Munich.

**1876** The first trams run in the city.

**1900** Munich becomes a centre of the Jugendstil (Art Nouveau) movement.

**1919** The assassination in Munich of Bavaria's first Prime Minister, Kurt Eisner, results in a communist republic.

## Living **Munich**

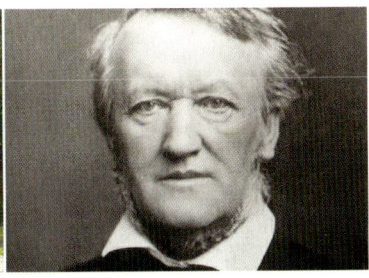

**1933** Hitler comes to power.

**1939** World War II commences.

**1940** First air attack on Munich (another 70 follow before 1945).

**1945** American troops take Munich.

**1946** Munich becomes the capital of the Free State of Bavaria.

**1972** A terrorist attack ends the 20th summer Olympic games in tragedy.

**1980** A bomb attack during the *Oktoberfest* claims 12 lives.

**1990** The reunification of Germany.

**1992** The World Economic Summit Meeting takes place in Munich. The new airport opens. Over 400,000 people participate in Germany's first *Lichterkette* (candle vigils) in Munich.

**2003** Munich celebrates 350 years of opera.

**2006** The opening ceremony and match of the World Cup is scheduled to take place on 9 June in Munich's new football stadium, which is due for completion May 2005.

Above left: *A memorial statue in the grounds of the notorious Dachau concentration camp*
Above: *Richard Wagner lived in Munich*

### RICHARD STRAUSS

Munich's greatest composer Richard Strauss was born in 1864, and eventually became the city's *Kapellmeister* (musical director). The breathtaking Bavarian scenery held a magnetic attraction for him, influencing his compositions considerably, and was particularly evident in his *Alpensinfonie*. His operas are still among the world's most popular and a fountain, depicting scenes from *Salome*, stands in the heart of the city as a memorial.

17

# Time to Shop

*Colourful puppets in the window of a Munich toyshop*

Munich's most popular shopping street is without doubt the pedestrian zone between Karlsplatz and Marienplatz; one kilometre (half a mile) of shopping fun with its huge department stores interspersed with boutiques and supermarkets. Even when the shops are closed this area is packed with window-shoppers. German fashions, leather and sportswear are all good buys. Just off Marienplatz, sports fans will revel in the giant sports department stores of Schuster and Sport Scheck (► 75), where you can buy everything from golf tees to skiing holidays.

Munich is the capital of Germany's fashion industry, and you will be amazed at the city's range of boutiques from haute couture and Bavarian *Trachten* (folk costume) to wacky new trends. In the elegant shops of Theatenerstrasse, Residenzstrasse and Maximilianstrasse famous designer labels rub shoulders with the classic Munich boutiques of Bogner and Rudolph Moshammer (► 78). Be sure to visit Loden-Frey (► 73), the largest shop for national costume in the world—look for articles in *Loden* cloth, a Bavarian speciality. This waterproof wool fabric in grey, navy or traditional green, has kept Münchners warm in winter for generations.

## CULINARY DELIGHTS

Local culinary specialities include countless types of sausage, best eaten with *Sußenf* (sweet mustard), as well as fine regional herbs, breads and cheese, all magnificently displayed on green wooden stalls at the traditional open-air Viktualienmarkt (► 75), while Dallmayr and Käfer (► 74) are among the finest delicatessens in Europe. For truly unique chocolates, visit Elly Seidl (► 74), famous for its *Münchner Küppeln* chocolates, shaped like the onion-domes of the Frauenkirche.

## Living **Munich**

As one of the world's leading publishing cities, with over 3,000 publishing houses, it is hardly surprising that Munich boasts a wide variety of bookshops, concentrated in the city's core and near the university in Schellingstrasse. Antiques shops, too, are popular, with many specializing in 'English', *Jugendstil* (art nouveau), and art deco styles. Collectors keep a look out for old Meissen or modern Rosenthal, while Nymphenburg porcelain—produced in Munich since 1747—is still manufactured in its traditional Rococo designs. For the finest in Bavarian handicrafts, visit the Kunstgewerbe-Verein in Pacellistrasse, or in the numerous streets converging on Max-Joseph-Platz, for unique Bavarian gifts, including hand-made puppets, carnival masks and porcelain beer steins.

No shopping spree would be complete without purchasing some of Munich's beer. The main breweries are Spaten-Franziskaner, Augustiner, Löwenbräu, Hacker-Pschoor, Hofbräuhaus and Paulaner. There are special glasses for special beers, special beers for certain seasons. And with beer halls everywhere, it won't take long to find out if you prefer *dunkles*, *Weissbier*, *Pills* or *helles*… As they say in Munich, *Prost*!

Middle: *Food hall of the Dallmayr Delicatessen*
Left: *A window full of local products*

### SPECIALIST SHOPS

Munich boasts a large number of small, old-fashioned shops that concentrate on one or two articles—for example, musical boxes, felt, buttons, knives, wood-carvings and even *Lederhosen*—and which are still to be found in the middle of town (➤ 76–77). Some of the best buys in Munich include German-made binoculars, telescopes, kitchenware, electronic gadgets and bed linen. The presence of so many top orchestras in Germany results in top-notch muscial instruments. Germany is also known for its manufacture of children's toys. You'll find everything from train sets and teddy-bears to traditional dolls and hand-made puppets.

# Out and About

**MORE IDEAS...**

**By Bike**
Spurwechsel (☎ 6 92 46 99) offer political or historical bike tours; also a 'nature' and a 'beer' tour. Cityhopper Touren (✉ Hohenzollernstrasse 95 ☎ 2 72 11 31) offer three cycle tours: the 2-hour 'Old Town Tour'; the 4-hour 'Romantic Tour' that takes in Munich's main parks; and a 'Valentin Tour' with stories from Karl Valentin (➤ 57).

**By Tram**
Stattreisen München (✉ Frauenlobstrassse 24 ☎ 54 40 42 30) offer the chance to explore Munich by tram.

**Out-of-town**
A number of tour operators offer excursions to nearby tourist attractions including day-trips to Neuschwanstein, Zugspitze (Germany's highest mountain), Berchtesgaden and Salzburg. Contact Panorama Tours (☎ 54 90 75 60) or Autobus Oberbayern (☎ 32 30 40).

*The grand concert hall of the late-19th-century Schloss Neuschwanstein*

## ORGANIZED SIGHTSEEING
Munich Tourist Office (✉ Sendlingerstrasse 1 ☎ 2 33 30–234) offers a range of tours that provide a thorough survey of the Bavarian metropolis. There are also custom tours that take a minimum of 2 hours.

Münchener Stadt-Rundfahrten (✉ Arnulfstrasse 8 ☎ 55 02 89 95) provide special night tours and city tours combined with the Bavaria Film Studios or the Olympiapark. Stattreisen München (✉ Frauenlobstrasse 24 ☎ 54 40 42 30) offers a variety of specialized walking tours including 'National Socialism and Resistance' detailing Munich's development as a Nazi capital; 'Munich and its Beer' explaining why Munich promotes itself as the Beer City; 'The Olympic Park and Village'; and 'Nymphenburg Castle' and Park.

## EXCURSIONS
### NEUSCHWANSTEIN
This fairy-tale castle is a magical white-turreted affair nestled in a pine forest in the foothills of the Bavarian Alps. In an attempt to make the fantasy world of Wagnerian opera a reality, 'Mad' King Ludwig commissioned a stage designer rather than an architect to design this romantic, theatrical castle, and watched it being built by telescope from his father's neighbouring castle. Only 15 of the 65 rooms were finished, and Ludwig only spent a few days there before he

# Living **Munich**

was dethroned. Fortunately, Ludwig's request to destroy the castle on his death was ignored and today it is Bavaria's number-one visitor attraction, and the lavish interior is worth lining up for, with its extravagant decor and vast wall paintings of Wagnerian scenes.

*The courtyard of the Schloss Herrenchiemsee*

### INFORMATION

**NEUSCHWANSTEIN**
**Distance** 120km (75 miles)
**Journey Time** About 2 hours
🕐 Guided tours 9–6 (summer), 10–4 (winter)
🚆 Daily excursions with Panorama Tours (► 20)
🛈 Münchenerstrasse 2, Schwangau
☎ (08362) 81980; www.neuschwanstein.de

## BAD TÖLZ
The beautiful spa town of Bad Tölz, at the foot of the Bavarian Alps, is famous for its iodine-rich springs and peat baths. The elegant cobbled main street, lined with handsome pastel-coloured houses ornately decorated with murals, leads up to the twin-spired Kreuzkirche noted for its Leonhard chapel. Bad Tölz is a perfect base for skiing and other mountain activities. Nearby Blombergbahn is Germany's longest summer toboggan run and the scene in winter of a crazy sled-flying competition.

### INFORMATION

**BAD TÖLZ**
**Distance** 40km (25 miles)
**Journey Time** 1 hour
🚆 Hourly trains from the main station
🛈 Max-Höfler-Platz 1
☎ (08041) 786717

## CHIEMSEE
Locally called the 'Bavarian Sea', Chiemsee is the largest of the Bavarian lakes. Its lush scenery and picture-postcard alpine backdrop has attracted artists for centuries and today draws holidaymakers to its shores for swimming, sailing and other pusuits. The lake's main attraction is Herrenchiemsee, site of Ludwig II's ambitious summer palace—a replica of the Château of Versailles. Only the central wing of the building was completed, including the spectacular Hall of Mirrors.

### INFORMATION

**CHIEMSEE**
**Distance** 80km (50 miles)
**Journey Time** 1 hour
🚆 Frequent trains to Prien from the main station
🕐 Guided palace tours 9–6 (summer), 9.40–4 (winter)
🛈 Alte Rathausstrasse 11, Prien am Chiemsee
☎ (08051) 69050 and (08051) 6090 (ferry); www.chiemseetourisms.de

# Walks

## INFORMATION

**Distance** 3km (1.8 miles)
**Time** 2 hours
**Start point**
★ Odeonsplatz
🚍 N24
Ⓤ U-Bahn Odeonplatz
**End point** Max-Joseph-Platz
🚍 K2
Ⓤ U-Bahn Odeonplatz

## MUNICH'S OLD TOWN

From Odeonsplatz walk down Brienner-strasse with its expensive antiques shops. After a short distance the elegant Wittelsbacherplatz opens out to the right, with an impressive equestrian statue of Elector Maximilian I. Soon afterwards, turn left at Amiraplatz, past the Greek Orthodox Salvatorkirche, and on into Kardinal-Faulhaber-Strasse where the distinctive domes of Frauenkirche tower over its spectacular façades. The Archbishop's Palace at No. 48 has been the residence of the archbishops of Munich and Freising since 1818. Turn into Promenadeplatz, past one of Munich's best hotels, the Bayerischer Hof (► 86), the Carmelite Church (the earliest baroque church in Munich) on your left and the Dreifaltigkeitskirche (Church of the Holy Trinity) opposite. Pass by Munich's Wittelsbach fountain (1885) at the main road, then turn left towards Mövenpick (► 70), one of the city's finest coffee houses.

Continue along the main road to Karlsplatz (Stachus). Pass through Karlstor (site of the former west gate to the city) into the pedestrian zone (Neuhauser Strasse). Don't miss the Michaelskirche (► 36), designed as a monument to the Counter-Reformation, before turning left on Augustinerstrasse to Munich's cathedral, the Frauenkirche (► 39). Return to the main shopping area via Liebfrauenstrasse and on to Marienplatz.

*The red-roofed late Gothic Frauenkirche, the Cathedral of Our Lady. The twin, onion-domed clock towers are characteristic Munich landmarks*

If you're feeling energetic, climb the Peterskirche tower (► 41)—the view of the city's sights is worth the effort. Swing round the side of the church to the Viktualienmarkt. Return to Marienplatz and walk up Dienerstrasse for a traditional Bavarian lunch in Spatenhaus (► 65) on Max-Joseph-Platz.

## Living **Munich**

### GARDENS & GALLERIES

Walk past the grand Residenz, home to the great Wittelsbach rulers and art collectors for five centuries, towards Odeonsplatz, then head eastwards into the enchanting Hofgarten (Court Garden), beautifully laid out with neat flowerbeds and fountains. Cut diagonally across the gardens, past the Staatskanzlei (State Chancellery) building, finished in 1994, and continue down a narrow path alongside the Finance Garden. Cross Von-der-Tann-Strasse by the pedestrian subway to the Haus der Kunst, an impressive modern art gallery, housed in a monumental building of the Third Reich.

The famous English Garden (►49) is just a stone's throw from the gallery. Head towards the Monopteros or Lovers' Temple, one of the park's great landmarks, for splendid views of Munich's skyline. Stop at the Chinese Tower, site of Munich's most popular beer garden, for light refreshment, then leave the English Garden in a westerly direction via Veterinärstrasse until you reach the university, marked by two magnificent bowl fountains. From here turn left into Ludwigstrasse, a grand avenue laid out by Ludwig I to display the wealth of his flourishing kingdom. The Ludwigskirche (Ludwig's Church; ►59) on your left contains one of the world's largest frescos.

Cross over Ludwigstrasse opposite the church into Schellingstrasse, just one of the maze of streets behind the university, bursting with student life in its many bars, cafés and shops. A left turn into Barerstrasse leads to Munich's three other great galleries: the Pinakothek der Moderne (►35), the Neue Pinakothek (►34) and the Alte Pinakothek (►33).

### INFORMATION

**Distance** 4km (2.5miles)
**Time** 2 hours
**Start point**
★ Max-Joseph-Platz
✚ N24
🚇 U-Bahn Odeonsplatz
**End point**
★ Alte Pinakothek
✚ M23
🚊 Tram 27

*The five-roofed Chinese Tower in Munich's popular English Garden*

# Munich by Night

*Outside tables at a Munich beer garden in the evening*

**AN EVENING STROLL**

Behind Marienplatz lies a maze of narrow lanes that have retained their medieval character. From the Old Town Hall, go down Burgstrasse, the oldest street in the city, past homes of former residents, Mozart and Cuvilliés. Go through the archway of the old royal residence (Alter Hof) and turn right past the Central Mint (Münzhof) along Pfisterstrasse to the royal brewery (Hofbräuhaus). Turn left up to the bright lights and dazzling designer windows of exclusive Maximiliansrasse, then left towards the magnificently illuminated Nationaltheater. Return along Dienerstrasse past Dallmayr—the former royal delicatessen—to Marienplatz.

Munich's nightlife is relatively small-scale and provincial compared to some cities. On a mild summer's evening, nothing beats strolling through the old town, seeing the illuminated historic buildings, or pausing to enjoy a drink or an ice cream on the broad sidewalk terraces of Leopoldstrasse. Eating and drinking in Munich are major pastimes, with wide ranging options from long, communal tables of the beer cellars to some of Germany's finest restaurants.

Munich is a city of music, with a famous operahouse long associated with Mozart, Wagner and Richard Strauss, and three major symphony orchestras. The Münchner Festspiele festival in July and August marks the musical highpoint of the year, attracting top international singers and opera aficionados. There's always something musical happening, from choral works and organ recitals in churches, open-air concerts in royal palaces, to live jazz, blues and rock venues, not to mention marionette-opera performances and even yodelling. If your German is good enough, Munich offers a dazzling programme of first-rate theatre, ranging from classical and contemporary productions to political cabaret.

Early-closing laws prevent many places from staying open all night, but Munich has plenty of vibrant bars and clubs, centred on Gärtnerplatz, the student district of Schwabing, and the Glockenbach quarter. Chose from foaming beer steins and drunken swaying to the oom-pah bands of the beer halls or the sophisticated cocktails in Germany's trendiest nightspots.

# MUNICH's
## top 25 sights

The sights are shown on the maps on the inside front cover and inside back cover, numbered **1**–**25** from west to east across the city

1. Schloss Nymphenburg *26*
2. Olympiapark *27*
3. BMW-Museum *28*
4. Dachau *29*
5. Schleissheim Palaces *30*
6. Lenbachhaus (City Gallery) *31*
7. Königsplatz *32*
8. Alte Pinakothek (Old Picture Gallery) *33*
9. Neue Pinakothek (New Picture Gallery) *34*
10. Pinakothek der Moderne (Modern Picture Gallery) *35*
11. Michaelskirche *36*
12. Asamkirche *37*
13. Münchner Stadtmuseum (Munich City Museum) *38*
14. Frauenkirche *39*
15. Neues Rathaus (New Town Hall) *40*
16. Peterskirche *41*
17. Spielzeugmuseum (Toy Museum) *42*
18. Viktualienmarkt *43*
19. Odeonsplatz *44*
20. Residenz *45*
21. Hofbräuhaus *46*
22. Nationaltheatre *47*
23. Deutsches Museum *48*
24. Englischer Garten (English Garden) *49*
25. Bayerisches Nationalmuseum (Bavarian National Museum) *50*

Top **25**

**1**

## Schloss Nymphenburg

### HIGHLIGHTS

- Amalienburg
- Badenburg
- Gallery of Beauties
- Porcelain Museum
- Magdalenenklause
- Marstallmuseum
- Botanical Garden

*Ornate coachwork in the Marstallmuseum*

### INFORMATION

- L18–19; Locator map off A2
- 17 90 80
- Palace Apr–mid-Oct daily 9–6; mid-Oct–end Mar daily 10–4. Botanical Gardens May–end Aug daily 6am–9.30pm; Sep–end Nov, Mar–end Apr daily 6am–7pm; Dec–end Feb daily 6.30–5.30
- Café Palmenhaus
- U-Bahn Rotkreuzplatz
- 41; tram 12, 17
- None ◪ Moderate
- Museum Mensch und Natur (▶ 62)

**It is hard to believe that one of Germany's largest baroque palaces, set in magnificent parkland, started life as a modest summer villa. This is one of Munich's loveliest areas.**

**The palace** Five generations of Bavarian royalty were involved in the construction of this vast palace, starting with Elector Ferdinand Maria. Thrilled by the birth of his heir Max Emanuel, he had the central section built in the style of an Italian villa by Agostino Barelli (1664–74) for his wife. Each succeeding ruler added to the building, resulting in a majestic, semicircular construction, stretching 500m (550yds) from one wing to the other.

**The interior** The central structure contains sumptuous galleries, including the majestic rococo Stone Hall and Ludwig I's Gallery of Beauties, featuring 36 Munich ladies, some said to have been the king's mistresses. In the old stables, the Marstallmuseum's dazzling collection of state carriages and sleighs recalls the heyday of the Wittelsbach family. The Porcelain Museum provides a comprehensive history of the famous Nymphenburg porcelain factory since its foundation in 1747.

**Park and pavilions** Originally in Italian then French baroque style, in 1803 Ludwig von Sckell transformed the gardens into a fashionable English park with ornate waterways, statues, pavilions and a maze. See yourself reflected 10-fold in the Hall of Mirrors in the Amalienburg hunting lodge, visit the unusual shell-encrusted Magdalenenklause hermitage and the Badenburg, said to be Europe's first post-Roman heated pool.

Top **25**

**2**

## Olympiapark

**Since the 1972 Olympics the park, with its intriguing skyline, has become one of the city's landmarks. Its tower offers an unforgettable view of Munich and the Alps.**

**The Games** The historic Oberwiesenfeld was a former royal Bavarian parade ground north of the city. In 1909 the world's first airship landed here, and from 1925 until 1939 it was Munich's airport. Used as a dump during World War II, it was transformed in 1968 into a multi-functional sport and recreation area. In 1972, it was the site of the 20th summer Olympic Games.

**The buildings** The television tower here, now called the Olympiaturm, built between 1965 and 1968, is the tallest reinforced concrete construction in Europe, and has become a symbol of modern Munich. When the weather is clear, the viewing platform and revolving restaurant give a breathtaking panorama of the Alps; the view of the city at night is magical. The tower's futuristic tent-roof looks like an immense spider's web; built at a cost of DM168 million, it is one of the most expensive roofs in the world. When you tour the area on a little train you will see the Olympiasee, a huge artificial lake; the Olympiaberg, a 53-m (174-ft) hill constructed from wartime rubble; the quaint Russian Orthodox chapel built by Father Timothy, a Russian recluse, beautifully decorated inside with thousands of pieces of silver paper; and the Olympic Village, remembered sadly today as the scene of the terrorist attack on 11 Israeli athletes on 5 September 1972.

### DID YOU KNOW?

- The Olympic park covers more than 3sq km (1sq mile)
- The Olympiaturm is 290m (950ft) high
- The Olympic Stadium, home to FC Bayern (▶ 85), holds 63,000 people
- The Olympic village houses about 9,000 people

### INFORMATION

**www**.olympiapark-muenchen.de

- J/K22; Locator map off A1
- Spiridon-Louis-Ring 21
- 30 67 27 07
- Olympiaturm daily 9–midnight. Olympiastadion Apr–end Oct daily 8.30–6; Nov–end Mar daily 9–4.30
- Revolving restaurant
- U-Bahn Olympiazentrum
- 36, 41, 43, 81, 136, 184

*The Olympiaturm*

Top **25**

**3**

# BMW-Museum

## HIGHLIGHTS

- 1899 Wartburg Motor Wagon
- 1923 R32 motorcycle
- 1931 Cabriolet
- 1934 Roadster
- 1936 BMW 328
- 1952 The 'Baroque Angel' (BMW 501)
- 1955 BMW 507 roadster

## INFORMATION

www.bmwmobiletradition.de
- J22; Locator map off A1
- Am Olympiaturm, Spiridon-Louis-Ring
- 38 22 33 07
- Apr–end Oct daily 10–10; Nov–end Mar daily 10–8
- U-Bahn Olympiazentrum
- 36, 41, 43, 81, 136, 184
- Excellent
- Moderate
- Olympiapark (▶ 27)
- Phone in advance for a factory tour, Apr–end Dec (38 22 33 06). Exhibits are constantly changing– phone in advance to avoid disappointment)

**Even if the world of automobiles doesn't particularly interest you, it's hard not to marvel at the developments of transport technology over the past five generations presented at this, the most popular company museum in Germany.**

**The museum** The BMW Time Horizon Museum, housed in a silvery, windowless half sphere, provides an eye-catching contrast to the adjacent high-rise headquarters of the Bavarian Motor Works (▶ 61). Over a quarter of a million visitors come to the BMW-Museum annually to see its fascinating display of rare cars and motorcycles, but regrettably, due to renovation work, the museum is currently closed until 2007. Highlights from the vehicle collection are on view in a smaller venue in the Globe at the Olympic Park. As well as vintage BMW models, there are also insights into the past through slides and videos covering such subjects as changing family life and work conditions, the role of women in industry and car recycling (where BMW is at the forefront of development).

**Future vision** Take a simulated journey into the future with electric or solar-generated hydrogen-drive cars or design your own model and watch it develop on computers. Adults and children vie with each other to sit in the cockpit of tomorrow's car and experiment with its sophisticated data and information systems. At the museum's cinema, a film Das weisse Phantom ('The White Phantom') about motorcycle race world champion Ernst Jakob Henne brings the world of motor-racing to life.

# Dachau

**Top 25**

**4**

**Once people visited Dachau to see the Renaissance château and town until it became synonymous with the Nazi reign of terror. Today the concentration camp (KZ-Gedenkstätte) has been preserved as a memorial to those who died here.**

**Summer castle** The pretty little town of Dachau, with its 18th-century pastel façades and quaint cobbled streets, is set on the steep bank of the Amper River. The Renaissance castle above the town, was once a popular summer residence of the Munich Royals. Only one wing of the original four survives; it contains a large banquet hall with one of the most exquisitely carved ceilings in Bavaria. Near by is the Dachauer Moos, a heath area often wreathed in mists, with a delicate light that is loved by artists.

**The camp** Münchners used to come to Dachau to wander its picturesque streets and visit the castle. But on 22 March 1933, only 50 days after Hitler came to power, Dachau was designated as the site of the first concentration camp of the Third Reich. Although it was not one of the main extermination camps, 31,951 deaths were recorded here between 1933 and 1945. Several of the original buildings have been restored as a memorial, a poignant reminder of the fate of the camp's 206,000 inmates. The museum documents the camp's history and the atrocities that happened here. The gates still bear the bitterly ironic slogan *'Arbeit macht frei'* ('Work makes you free').

## INFORMATION

- www.kz-gedenkstatte-dachau.de
- Off map to northwest; Locator map off A1
- S-Bahn Dachau

**The Concentration Camp**
- Alte Römerstrasse 75
- (08131) 66 99 70
- Daily 9–5
- S-Bahn to Dachau, then 726 to KZ-Gedenkstätte Haupteingang or 724 to KZ-Gedenkstätte Parkplatz
- Excellent  Free

*Memorial to the dead*

DEN TOTEN ZUR EHR DEN LEBENDEN ZUR MAHNUNG

Top **25**

**5**

## Schleissheim Palaces

**These three palaces capture the splendour of Munich's past. Make sure you see the Great Gallery, the charming French-style gardens and the magnificent display of Meissen porcelain.**

**Old Palace** In 1597 Duke Wilhelm V bought a farm to the east of the Dachau moor as a retirement residence. His son, Prince Elector Maximilian I, later transformed it into an Italian-style Renaissance palace, and called it the Altes Schloss Schleissheim. Today it contains part of the Bavarian National Museum, including an unusual gallery devoted to international religious folk art.

**New Palace** The beautiful Neues Schloss, the 'Versailles of Munich', was commissioned by Prince Elector Max Emanuel II as a summer residence. The largest palace complex of its day, it demonstrated his wealth and power. Despite severe damage during World War II, the sumptuous rococo interior remains largely intact. The Great Gallery, over 60m (197ft) long, contains the Bavarian State Art Collection. One of the most remarkable collections of baroque paintings in Europe, it has around a thousand paintings, including masterpieces by Rubens, Titian, Veronese and van Dyck.

**Palace Lustheim** Separated from the New Palace by delightful formal gardens and encircled by a decorative canal, Palace Lustheim (Schloss Lustheim) was originally accessible only by boat. Planned as an island of happiness for Max Emanuel's bride Maria Antonia, it now houses Germany's largest collection of Meissen porcelain.

### HIGHLIGHTS

**Old Palace**
- Religious folk art

**New Palace**
- Great Gallery

**Palace Lustheim**
- Meissen Porcelain Museum

### INFORMATION

- ✚ Off map to north; Locator map off A1
- ☎ Old Palace 3 15 52 72. New/Lustheim 3 15 87 20
- 🕐 Apr–end Sep Tue–Sun 9–6; Oct–end Mar 10–4
- Ⓢ S-Bahn Oberschleissheim
- 🚌 292    ♿ None
- 💰 Old Palace inexpensive; New/Lustheim moderate; combined ticket expensive

*Meissen chinoiserie, Schloss Lustheim*

Top **25**

**6**

## Lenbachhaus

**This beautiful city gallery displays predominantly 19th- and 20th-century works of art. The tiny formal garden is also a delight—a blend of modern and classical statuary and fountains.**

**The Lenbachhaus** This charming villa was built in 1887 in Florentine High Renaissance style by Gabriel von Seidl for the 'painter prince' Franz von Lenbach, darling of the German aristocracy and the most fashionable Bavarian painter of his day. After his death, it became the property of the city and was converted into the municipal art gallery (Städtische Galerie im Lenbachhaus). A north wing was added in the late 1920s to balance the south wing, where Lenbach's studio was housed. The resulting structure perfectly frames the terrace and ornamental gardens.

**The collections** The chief objective of the City Gallery is to document the development of painting in Munich from the late Gothic period up to the present day. Munich Romantics and landscape artists, including Spitzweg, Leibl, Defregger, Lenbach and Corinth are well represented, as is the Jugendstil period. However, it is the paintings by the Munich-based expressionist group known as *Der Blaue Reiter* (Blue Rider) that gained the Lenbachhaus international fame, including over 300 works by Wassily Kandinsky, who founded the movement with Franz Marc. Paul Klee, Gabriele Münter, August Macke and Alexej von Jawlensky are well represented, and the collection of contemporary art by Anselm Kiefer, Andy Warhol, Roy Lichtenstein, Josef Beuys and others is dazzling.

### HIGHLIGHTS

- Kandinsky collection
- *Der Blaue Reiter* collection
- *Show your Wounds*, Joseph Beuys
- *Blue Horse*, Franz Marc
- Munich Jugendstil collection

*The formal Italian garden. Top:* Jawlensky und Werefkin *by Münter*

### INFORMATION

**www.**lenbachhaus.de
- M23; Locator map A2
- Luisenstrasse 33
- 23 33 20 00
- Tue–Sun 10–6
- Café and garden terrace
- U-Bahn Königsplatz
- Good
- Expensive
- *Der Blaue Reiter* guided tours occasionally organized by the Munich Volkshochschule

# Top 25

## 7

# Königsplatz

## HIGHLIGHTS

**Glyptothek**
- Barberinian Faun (*above*)
- Mnesarete tomb relief
- Aeginetan marbles
- Crowned bust of Emperor Augustus
- Mosaic pavement from Sentinum
- Boy with a goose

**Staatliche Antikensammlung**
- Exekesias and Dionysus kraters
- Funeral wreath of Armento

## INFORMATION

- M23; Locator map B2
- Königsplatz
- Glyptothek 28 61 00. Antikensammlung 59 98 88 30
- Glyptothek Tue–Sun 10–5 (Tue, Thu until 8). Antikensammlung Tue, Thu–Sun 10–5, Wed 10–8
- Glyptothek museum café
- U-Bahn Königsplatz
- Good (Glyptothek); none (Antikensammlung)
- Moderate
- Lenbachhaus (➤ 31), Alte Pinakothek (➤ 33), Neue Pinakothek (➤ 34)
- Free guided tour Wed 6pm at the Antikensammlung and Thu 6pm at the Glyptothek

**Three immense neo-classical temples, including the Propyläen, modelled on the Athenian Acropolis, flank this spacious, majestic square, nicknamed Athens-on-the-Isar, lending it an air of grandeur reminiscent of an ancient forum.**

**The Square and the Propyläen** Along with the buildings of Ludwigstrasse, Königsplatz represents Ludwig I's greatest contribution to Munich. Laid out by Leo von Klenze, according to plans created by Carl von Fischer, the square took 50 years to complete, from 1812 to 1862. The final building, the Propyläen, is the most striking.

**Nazi control** Between 1933 and 1935, the appearance of Königsplatz was completely transformed. Hitler paved over the grass-covered, tree-lined square and Königsplatz became the National Socialists' 'Akropolis Germaniae'—an impressive setting for Nazi rallies. The paving stones have been replaced by broad expanses of lawn, and Königsplatz is serene once again.

**Museums** The Glyptothek, or Sculpture Museum, on the north flank of Königsplatz is the oldest museum in Munich and one of the most celebrated neo-classical buildings in Germany. Inside is one of Europe's foremost collections of ancient Greek and Roman sculpture. To the south, the Corinthian-style Staatliche Antikensammlung (State Collection of Antiquities) has a priceless collection of ancient vases, jewellery, bronzes and terracotta sculptures.

Top **25**

**8**

## Alte Pinakothek

**With its more than 850 Old Master paintings this massive museum, the Old Picture Gallery, is rated alongside the Louvre, Uffizi, Prado and the Metropolitan as one of the world's most important galleries. The Rubens Collection alone is the finest on earth.**

**Architectural masterpiece** The pinnacle of Bavaria's centuries-old dedication to the arts, the gallery was commissioned by Ludwig I and designed by Leo von Klenze to replace the older Kammergalerie in the Residenz, which had become too small for the Royal Collection. Modelled on the Renaissance palaces of Venice, it took ten years to construct and on completion in 1836 was proclaimed a masterpiece—the largest gallery building of its time and a model for other museum buildings in Rome and Brussels. During World War II it was so badly damaged that demolition of the site was contemplated. Restored in the 1950s and given an extensive face-lift in the 1990s, the magnificent gallery provides a wonderful backdrop for one of the world's finest collections of Western paintings.

**Priceless treasures** All the main schools of European art from the Middle Ages to the beginning of the 19th century are represented, with the emphasis on German, Dutch and Flemish paintings, including works by Dürer, van Dyck, Rembrandt and Breughel, and more than 100 pieces by Rubens.

### HIGHLIGHTS

- *Fool's Paradise*, Pieter Breughel the Elder
- *Four Apostles*, Dürer
- *Adoration of the Magi*, Tiepolo
- *Madonna Tempi*, Raphael
- *The Great Last Judgement*, Rubens
- *The Resurrection*, Rembrandt

### INFORMATION

**www**.alte-pinakothek.de
- M23; Locator map B1
- Barerstrasse 27
- 23 80 52 16
- Tue–Sun 10–5 (Tue until 8)
- U-Bahn Theresienstrasse
- Tram 27
- Very good   Expensive; Sun free
- Neue Pinakothek (➤ 34), Pinakothek der Moderne (➤ 35)

*Dürer's* Four Apostles

33

Top **25**

**9**

## Neue Pinakothek

### HIGHLIGHTS

- *Ostende,* William Turner
- *Breakfast,* Edouard Manet
- *Vase with Sunflowers* and *View of Arles,* Vincent van Gogh
- *Large Reclining Woman,* Henry Moore

The Laundress *Degas*

### INFORMATION

**www.neue-pinakothek.de**
- M23; Locator map C1
- Barerstrasse 29
- 23 80 51 95
- Wed–Mon 10–5 (Wed until 8)
- Café with terrace
- U-Bahn Theresienstrasse
- Tram 27
- Very good   Expensive
- Alte Pinakothek (➤ 33), Pinakothek der Moderne (➤ 35)

**The New Picture Gallery is a shining contrast to the Renaissance-style Old Picture Gallery across the road; it houses collections through the 19th and early 20th centuries.**

**Palazzo Branca** As with the Old Picture Gallery (Alte Pinakothek), it was Ludwig I who instigated the building of this gallery as a home for contemporary art in 1846. However, it was damaged extensively during World War II, so a competition was held in 1966 to design a new gallery in the heart of Schwabing, Munich's trendy student quarter.

**Successful design** The winning entry, by Munich architect Alexander von Branca, was built at a staggering cost of DM105 million and was opened in 1981. The attractive concrete, granite and glass structure, sometimes known as the Palazzo Branca, integrates art-deco and post-modernist designs with traditional features in an unusual figure-of-eight formation around two inner courtyards and terraced ponds.

**Art treasures** The Neue Pinakothek contains over 1,000 paintings, drawings and sculptures spanning a variety of periods from rococo to Jugendstil, focusing on the development of German art alongside English 19th-century landscapes and portraits, and French Impressionism. It is best to follow the 22 rooms in chronological order, starting with early Romantic works, then on through French and German late Romanticism to French and German Impressionism, with major works by Manet, Monet, Bonnard and Klimt.

Top **25**

**10**

## Pinakothek der Moderne

**With four major museums under one roof, the Pinakothek der Moderne, founded in 2002, is regarded as one of the world's greatest collections of 20th- and 21st-century art.**

**State Gallery of Modern Art** Modern art occupies half of the total exhibition space in the Pinakothek, with an exceptional display of paintings, sculptures, video installations and photographic art, plus incomparable collections of German Expressionism and Surrealism. Works by Magritte, Picasso, Dalí and Warhol characterize 20th-century art movements, while more recent trends are represented by Rist, Falvin and Wall.

**The New Collection** This is one of the leading international collections of applied modern arts—a veritable treasure trove of over 50,000 items illustrating the history of design, with exhibits ranging from cars to computers and from robots to running shoes. The exhibits are arranged chronologically with highlights including the avant-garde of the 1920s and 1930s, functionalism, Pop-Art design and the space euphoria of the 1960s.

**Architecture Museum** The largest collection of its kind in Germany, comprising drawings, photographs and models of over 700 international architects, displayed in temporary exhibitions on such themes as German architecture and current trends.

**State Graphic Art Collection** In rooms alongside the Architecture Museum you can see selections from the State Graphics Collection, which boasts over 4000,000 etchings and drawings spanning seven centuries.

### HIGHLIGHTS

- *World Peace Projected*, Bruce Nauman
- *Madame Soler*, Pablo Picasso
- *The End of the 20th Century*, Joseph Beuys
- *The Starting Line*, with installations by Metzel, Grimonprez, Rist, Dijkstra, Bock and others
- The *Entartete Kunst* ('Degenerate Art') collection
- Bauhaus furniture
- Bent-wood furniture
- Mobile phone collection

### INFORMATION

**www.**pinakothek-der-moderne.de
- M23; Locator C1
- Barerstrasse 40
- 23 80 53 60
- Tue–Sun 10–5 (Thu–Fri until 8)
- Café-bistro
- U-Bahn Königsplatz or Theresienstrasse
- 53; tram 27
- Very good
- Expensive; Sun free
- Alte Pinakothek (➤ 33), Neue Pinakothek (➤ 34)
- Day pass available for all three Pinakothek Museums. Free guided tours

35

Top **25**

**11**

# Michaelskirche

## HIGHLIGHTS

- High Altar
- *St. Michael fighting the Devil*, Christoph Schwarz
- Four bronze reliefs, Hubert Gerhard
- Reliquary shrine of saints Cosmos and Damian
- *Mary Magdalen at the feet of Christ Crucified*, Giovanni da Bologna
- *Annunciation*, Peter Candid

## INFORMATION

- **www.** jesuiten.org/st-michael
- N23; Locator map B3
- Neuhauser Strasse 52
- 2 31 70 60
- Mon–Sat 10–7 (Thu until 8.45), Sun 6.50am–10.15pm
- U- or S-Bahn Karlsplatz
- Tram 16, 17, 18, 19, 20, 21, 27  None

**It is easy to miss the Michaelskirche, hidden amidst the smart boutiques and department stores of the main shopping precinct, but behind its striking façade lies the largest Renaissance church north of the Alps.**

**Eventful construction** The Jesuit Church of St. Michael was built at the end of the 16th century by Duke Wilhelm (the Pious) as a monument to the Counter-Reformation. Disaster struck in 1590 when the tower collapsed; it was finally consecrated in 1597. War damage has been masterfully repaired and you will marvel at the Renaissance hall with its ornate, barrel-vaulted roof.

**The façade** The bold late-Renaissance façade is unified by the consistency of rounded windows, doorways and niches. In the true combative spirit of the Counter-Reformation, these niches contain stone figures of the Wittelsbach dukes and emperors—secular defenders of the faith—including a splendid figure of the church's patron, Wilhelm V. The large ground-level niche shows St. Michael triumphing over the devil. The highest niche is reserved for Christ.

**Impressive interior** A further depiction of the Archangel Michael forms the altarpiece of the soaring, three-storey altar erected by Sustris, Dietrich and Schwarz (1586–89). However, the most dominant architectural feature is the triumphal arch at the entrance to the choir—symbolizing the victory of the Counter-Reformation and echoed in the arches of the transepts, side chapels and galleries. The Royal Crypt contains the tombs of 41 members of the Wittelsbach family.

## Asamkirche

**The Asamkirche may be Munich's finest rococo structure. The narrow but sensational façade provides a mere hint of the sumptuous interior—one of the most lavish works of the celebrated Asam brothers.**

**The Asam brothers** In 1729, master architect and sculptor Ägid Quirin Asam acquired a house in Sendlingerstrasse and built his own private church next door, assisted by his brother, a distinguished fresco artist. For this reason, the Church of St. John Nepomuk (a Bohemian saint popular in 18th-century Bavaria) is better known as the Asamkirche. Even though Asam financed the construction, he was forced to open it to the public, and the church was consecrated in 1746. Free from the normal constraints of a patron's demands, the brothers created a dazzling jewel of rococo architecture.

**Lavish decoration** The unobtrusive marble façade has an unusual plinth of unhewn rocks and a kneeling figure of St. John Nepomuk. Upon entering you are immediately struck by the breathtaking opulence of the tiny, dark interior, crammed with sculptures, murals and gold leaf, and crowned by a magnificent ceiling fresco depicting the life of the saint. The long, narrow nave, with its encircling gallery and projecting moulded cornice, carries your eye straight to the glorious two-tiered high altar and shrine of St. John Nepomuk. The gleaming gallery altar, portraying the Trinity and illuminated by an oval window representing the sun, is crowned by Ägid Quirin's *Throne of Mercy*, depicting Christ crucified, in the arms of God, wearing the papal crown.

### Top 25
**12**

### HIGHLIGHTS

- *Gnadenstuhl (Throne of Mercy)*, Ä. Q. Asam
- Ceiling fresco, C D Asam
- Two-tiered High Altar
- Wax effigy of St. John Nepomuk
- Statues of John the Baptist and St. John the Evangelist
- Portraits of the Asam brothers
- Façade

### INFORMATION

- N23; Locator map B3
- Sendlinger Strasse 62
- 23 68 79 89
- Daily 8–5.30
- U-Bahn Sendlinger Tor
- 31, 56; tram 16, 17, 18, 27
- None
- Münchner Stadtmuseum (▶ 38), Münchner Marionettentheater (▶ 82)
- Free tours (in German) Thu at 4pm

Top **25**

**13**

# Münchner Stadtmuseum

## HIGHLIGHTS

- History of the city section
- Marionette Theatre Collection and fairground museum
- Photography and Film Museum

*Puppet in the City Museum*

## INFORMATION

**www.**stadtmuseum-online.de
- N23; Locator map C3
- St.-Jakobs-Platz 1
- 23 32 23 70
- Tue–Sun 10–6
- Café and beer garden
- U-Bahn Sendlinger Tor, U- or S-Bahn Marienplatz
- 52, 56
- Good
- Inexpensive
- Tours, lectures

**Munich's unique, lively, eclectic personality is reflected in the diverse nature of the City Museum's collections, which range from weapons, armour and fashion to fairgrounds, Biedermeier and films.**

**City history** If your itinerary does not allow enough time to explore all the old parts of the city on foot, head straight to the History of the City section housed on the first floor, to study Munich's development since the Middle Ages through maps, models and before-and-after-photographs, which illustrate the devastating effects of World War II bombing.

**Unusual collections** As the museum is housed in the former city armoury, it is only fitting that it should contain one of the largest collections of ancient weaponry in Germany. Other collections worth visiting include fashion from the 18th century to the present day, the second-largest musical instrument collection in Europe and the Photography and Film Museum, with its fascinating display of ancient cameras and photographs. Don't miss the greatest treasure—Erasmus Grasser's 10 *Morris Dancers* (1480), magnificent examples of late Gothic secular art, originally carved for the Old Town Hall (➤ 42).

**For children of all ages** On the third floor, everyone loves the Marionette Theatre Collection (Münchner Marionettentheater ➤ 82), one of the world's largest, reflecting Bavaria's role in the production of glove-puppets, shadow plays and mechanical toys. The fairground museum is most enjoyable too. Look out for the moving King Kong.

Top **25**

# 14

## Frauenkirche

**This massive, late Gothic brick church symbolizes Munich more than any other building. Its sturdy twin towers (99m/325ft and 100m/328ft high), with their Italian-Renaissance onion domes, dominate the city's skyline.**

**Munich's cathedral** The Frauenkirche, built between 1468 and 1488, has been the cathedral of Southern Bavaria since 1821. Today's structure, the largest reconstructed medieval building in Munich, has been rebuilt from the rubble of World War II. Little remains of the original design except the basic architectural elements and the windows in the choir. Its strength lies in its simplicity and grand proportions.

**Onion domes** Thirty years after the church's consecration, the towers were still roofless. In 1524, unique green Italian-Renaissance onion domes were erected as a temporary measure. With this eccentric addition to the structure, the building once provoked an irreverent comparison to a pair of beer mugs with lids. However, the domes became so popular, that they were retained.

**The Devil's Footprint** A footprint is visible in the stone floor by the entrance. Legend has it that the Devil visited the church and stamped his foot in delight because the architect had apparently forgotten to put in windows, though the building was flooded with light. But Jörg von Halsbach's ingenious design meant that no windows were visible from this point, thus giving him the last laugh.

### HIGHLIGHTS

- Gothic stained-glass windows
- *The Baptism of Christ*, Friedrich Pacher altarpiece
- Jan Polack altar panels
- St. Lantpert's Chapel with wood figures of apostles and prophets from the workshop of Erasmus Grasser

*The Frauenkirche's twin onion-domed spires*

### INFORMATION

- N23; Locator map C3
- Frauenplatz 1
- 29 00 82-0
- South Tower Apr–end Oct Mon–Sat 10–5
- U- or S-Bahn Marienplatz
- 52; tram 19
- None
- Moderate
- Neue Rathaus (➤ 40), Spielzeugmuseum (➤ 42)

Top **25**

**15**

# Neues Rathaus

## HIGHLIGHTS

- Glockenspiel
- Façade
- Tower
- Ratskeller (➤ 65)

## INFORMATION

- N24; Locator map C3
- Marienplatz
- 2 33 03 00
- Tower Mon–Thu 9–4, Fri 9–1
- Ratskeller beer hall and restaurant (➤ 65)
- U- or S-Bahn Marienplatz
- 52
- Few
- Tower: Inexpensive
- Frauenkirche (➤ 39), Peterskirche (➤ 41), Spielzeugmuseum (➤ 42), Viktualienmarkt (➤ 43)

**Eleven o'clock is the magic hour for tourists who crowd Marienplatz to see the world-famous Munich Glockenspiel in action on the lavish neo-Gothic façade of the New Town Hall.**

**Towers and turrets** The imposing New Town Hall, seat of the city government for nearly a century, dominates the entire north side of Marienplatz, and is traditionally the scene of tournaments, festivals and ceremonies. Constructed between 1867 and 1909 around six courtyards with towers and turrets, sculptures and gargoyles, its neo-Gothic style was controversial at the time, but the Neues Rathaus has since become one of Munich's best-known landmarks.

**The Glockenspiel** On the main front of the building, figures of Bavarian royalty stand alongside saints and characters from local folklore. The central tower viewing platform offers a fantastic view of the city centre, and houses one of the largest Glockenspiels (carillons) in Europe. This mechanical clock plays four different tunes on 43 bells while 32 almost life-sized carved figures present scenes from Munich's history—among them the jousting match at the marriage of Duke Wilhelm V with Renate of Lorraine in 1568, and the *Schäfflertanz* (Coopers' dance) of 1517, celebrating the end of the Black Death. This dance is re-enacted in Munich's streets every seven years (next in 2011). Both Glockenspiel events can be seen daily at 11am and also at noon and at 5pm in summer. The cuckoo that ends the performance always raises a smile.

Top **25**

# 16

## Peterskirche

**Known affectionately to Münchners as 'Alter Peter', the city's oldest parish church is immortalized in a traditional song that claims 'Until Old Peter's tower falls down, we'll have a good life in Munich town'.**

**Built over time** The Peterskirche dates from the foundations of the city itself in 1158, on a slight hill called the Petersbergl, where the monks (who gave their name to Munich) had established a settlement in the 11th century. The original Romanesque structure was expanded in Gothic style, and remodelled along Renaissance lines in the 17th century, when the famous tower with its lantern-dome was created.

**Destruction and rebirth** During World War II the church was almost entirely destroyed. In an attempt to raise money to rebuild it, Bavarian Radio stirred the hearts of the people of Munich by playing only a shortened version of the 'Alter Peter' song, and public donations flowed in. After the tower was completed, in October 1951, the full version was at last heard again.

**Bells and a view** The most extraordinary feature of the tower is its eight asymmetrically placed clock-faces, designed so that, according to Munich comedian Karl Valentin, eight people can tell the time at once. The chimes are renowned and include one of the largest bells in Germany: The best time to hear them is at 3pm on Saturday, when they ring in the Sabbath. The 306-step climb to the viewing platform is rewarded by a dramatic bird's-eye view of Munich with its magnificent Alpine backdrop.

## HIGHLIGHTS

- High Altar (Nikolaus Stuber, Ägid Quirin Asam and Erasmus Grasser)
- Clock tower
- Schrenk Altar
- Jan Polack's five Gothic pictures
- Mariahilf Altar (Ignaz Günther)
- Corpus-Christi Altar (Ignaz Günther)
- Aresinger-Epitaph (Erasmus Grasser)

## INFORMATION

- N24; Locator map C3
- Petersplatz
- 2 60 48 28
- Tower Mon–Sat 9–6, Sun 10–6 (until 7 in summer). Closed in bad weather
- U- or S-Bahn Marienplatz
- 52
- None
- Tower inexpensive
- Neues Rathaus (➤ 40), Spielzeugmuseum (➤ 42), Viktualienmarkt (➤ 43)

Top **25**

**17**

## Spielzeugmuseum

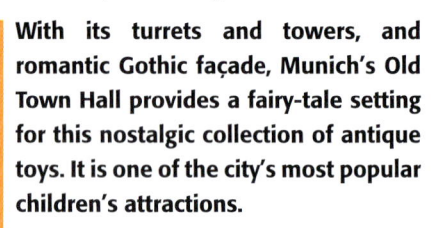

**With its turrets and towers, and romantic Gothic façade, Munich's Old Town Hall provides a fairy-tale setting for this nostalgic collection of antique toys. It is one of the city's most popular children's attractions.**

*Clock on the Old Town Hall*

### HIGHLIGHTS

- Steiff teddy bears
- Hauser-Elastolin collection
- Smallest doll in the world
- Jumping jacks from Oberammergau
- Moscovian painted puppets
- Model Zeppelin
- First ever Bakelite toy television

### INFORMATION

- N24; Locator map D3
- Im Alten Rathausturm, Marienplatz
- 29 40 01
- Daily 10–5.30
- U- or S-Bahn Marienplatz
- 52
- None
- Moderate

**Toys galore** It's easy to miss the tiny entrance to the Toy Museum, hidden at the foot of the Altes Rathaus' (Old Town Hall) grand Gothic tower of the southeast corner of Marienplatz. From here, a narrow spiral staircase leads up to four floors of neatly arranged European and American toys dating from the last two centuries.

**Old and new** Start with the teddy bears, toy soldiers, dolls and model cars belonging to local caricaturist Ivan Steiger at the top and work your way down, tracing the history of toys, starting with old dolls, animals and folk toys dating back to 1780, from Bohemia, Vienna, Russia and other famous European toy-making centres. Don't miss the folk toys from Berchtesgaden, the world's smallest doll and the celebrated Steiff teddy bears.

**Dolls and carousels** Lower down the tower, a splendid collection of carousels and steam engines is followed by part of the Hauser-Elastolin archive collection, named after one of Germany's main toy producers, and a series of American toys made famous in Europe in comics, among them Felix the Cat and Humpty Dumpty, and other childhood favourites. The second floor contains a series of sophisticated model train layouts, and the first floor has a fine collection of dolls and dolls' houses.

Top **25**

# 18

## Viktualienmarkt

**Less than a stone's throw from the cosmopolitan shops of Munich's main pedestrian zone, this bustling open-air food market, with taverns and cooked food stands, has retained its traditional atmosphere for centuries.**

**A long tradition** In 1807 it was decided that the market in Marienplatz had become too small for the rapidly growing trade. So a new Viktualienmarkt was planned for a grassy field outside the city, where livestock grazed and stage-coaches stopped. Today it is Munich's oldest, largest and most attractive market with its quaint green wooden stalls and colourful striped umbrellas.

**Atmosphere** The lively atmosphere of the market owes much to the robust market women, famous for the loud and colourful abuse they dish out to their customers. Dare to haggle over the price or quality of their produce and you will be scolded in an earthy Bavarian dialect you won't understand, but you'll get the message. Their goods are superb, the prices high and the variety of fresh produce is vast, ranging from Bavarian blue cheese to Alpine herbs and flowers. Look out for neatly tied bundles of asparagus in spring, and mountains of freshly picked cranberries in summer.

**Open-air restaurant** Try some Bavarian specialities from the little taverns and stands dotted around the market—*Leberkäs* (meat loaf) or a *Brat-* or *Weisswürst* (white sausage)—wash it down with a typically Bavarian *Weissbier* in the beer garden set up round the maypole, the scene of lively May Day celebrations.

*Viktualienmarkt's maypole*

### HIGHLIGHTS

- Rottler—over 40 different kinds of potato
- Natursaft Müller—freshly pressed fruit juices
- Lebküchen Schmidt—spiced biscuits (➤ 75)
- Münchner Suppenküche —soup kitchen (➤ 71)
- Nordsee—fish snacks (➤ 71)
- Pferdemetzger—speciality horsemeat sausages
- Kräuterstand Freisinger—herbs and spices
- Honighäusl—herbal honey wines

### INFORMATION

- N24; Locator map D3
- Mon–Fri 7.30–6, Sat 7.30–1
- Numerous stands serve hot and cold snacks
- U- or S-Bahn Marienplatz
- 52
- Neues Rathaus (➤ 40), Peterskirche (➤ 41), Spielzeugmuseum (➤ 42), Valentin Museum (➤ 57)

Top **25**

**19**

# Odeonsplatz

## HIGHLIGHTS

- Theatinerkirche (➤ 59)
- Feldherrnhalle
- Hofgarten
- Leuchtenberg-Palais
- Odeon
- Ludwig I monument
- Preysing Palais
- Staatskanzlei (➤ 61)

## INFORMATION

- N24; Locator map D2
- Hofgarten Café
- U-Bahn Odeonsplatz
- 53
- Residenz (➤ 45), Haus der Kunst (➤ 56), Englischer Garten (➤ 49)

*The Hofgarten and Theatinerkirche, burial place of the Wittelsbachs*

**Monumental buildings surround this square at the start of the city's two finest boulevards. Rubbing the noses of the lions guarding the entrance to the Residenz brings good luck.**

**Grand plan for urban expansion** Ludwig I entrusted the layout of Odeonsplatz to Leo von Klenze in the early 19th century to demonstrate the wealth of his flourishing kingdom. It also shows Klenze's passion for Renaissance Italy. His neo-classical Leuchtenberg-Palais (today the Bavarian Ministry of Finance) was inspired by Rome's Palazzo Farnese, and set the pattern for the development of the magnificent Lugwigstrasse.

**Felderrnhalle** Apart from the striking Theatinerkirche (➤ 59)—Bavaria's first baroque building and for many the most beautiful church in Munich—perhaps the most imposing building in Odeonsplatz is the Felderrnhalle (Military Commander's Hall), commissioned by Ludwig I, and designed by Freidrich von Gärtner, as a tribute to the Bavarian army, and adorned with statues of Bavarian generals. Note the faces of the two bronze lions: One is said to be growling at the Residenz while the other, facing the church, remains silent.

**The Court Garden** The peaceful Hofgarten—a park beside Odeonsplatz—retains its original 17th-century Italian layout of beautifully tended flowerbeds and fountains. The garden is enclosed on two sides by long arcades housing galleries and cafés, and by the impressive Staatskanzlei (➤ 61) building to the east.

Top **25**

**20**

# Residenz

**The glittering state rooms of this magnificent palace demonstrate the power and wealth of the Wittelsbach dynasty —five centuries of dukes, prince-electors and kings.**

**Historical evolution** Despite devastating damage in World War II, the Residenz was painstakingly reconstructed over four decades to its original state: a harmonious fusion of Renaissance, baroque, rococo and neo-classical styles. As you explore the 112 grand rooms crammed with priceless treasures, you can trace the centuries of architectural development, as well as the history and lifestyles of the great Wittelsbach family dynasty.

**Palace highlights** It would take a full day to see everything; if time is limited just see the Ahnengalerie (Ancestral Portrait Gallery), hung with paintings of 121 members of the Wittelsbach family; the Hofkapelle and the Reiche Kapelle, two intimate chapels (one for the courtiers and the other for the royal family); the Brunnenhof courtyard with its magnificent fountain; the unusual shell-encrusted Grottenhof courtyard; and the Antiquarium, the largest Renaissance vaulted hall in northern Europe.

**Jewel in the crown** The truly dazzling Cuvilliés Theatre, jewel of the Residenz and the finest rococo theatre in the world, is a truly dazzling spectacle. Built in 1750, it hosted the première of Mozart's *Idomeneo* in 1781. Also, visit the Treasury (Schatzkammer) to see the crown jewels and one of the most valuable collections of ecclesiastical and secular treasures in Europe, spanning a thousand years.

## HIGHLIGHTS

- Cuvilliés Theatre
- Schatzkammer
- Antiquarium
- Ahnengalerie
- Hofkapelle
- Egyptian Art Museum
- Coin Museum

*The splendid ceiling of the Antiquarium*

## INFORMATION

- N24; Locator map D2
- Residenzstrasse/Max-Joseph-Platz 3
- 29 06 71
- Daily 10–4 (6 in summer)
- U- or S-Bahn Marienplatz, U-Bahn Odeonsplatz
- 53; tram 19
- Good
- Expensive; Schatzkammer expensive; Cuvilliés Theatre moderate
- Tours daily. Separate tour for the Schatzkammer

45

Top **25**

**21**

# Hofbräuhaus

### DID YOU KNOW?

- The Hofbräuhaus is the world's most famous pub
- The Munich Beer Regulations of 1487 are the oldest written food laws in the world
- Bavaria contains more than a sixth of the world's 4,000 breweries
- The biggest beer gardens in Germany can be found in Munich: the 200-year-old Hirschgarten offers seating for 8,500 guests, the Chinesischer Turm seats 7,000 and the Augustiner-Keller has 5,000 seats

### INFORMATION

- www.hofbrauhaus.de
- N24; Locator map D3
- Am Platzl 9
- 29 01 36 0
- Daily 9–midnight. Brass band 11am–3pm, 5.30–midnight
- U- or S-Bahn Marienplatz
- 52; tram 19
- Good

**No trip to Munich is complete without a visit to the Hofbraühaus, despite its being a tourist honeypot, to sip a cool beer in the shady courtyard or in the lively beer hall. The Hofbräuhaus was founded by Wilhelm V in 1589.**

**Royal beer** The brewery produced a special dark ale for Wilhelm's court, because he disliked the expensive local beer. Beer in Bavaria had been considered an aristocratic drink ever since the harsh winters of the 14th century destroyed the Bavarian vineyards. The ordinary citizens were unable to taste this royal brew until 1828, when the brewery finally became an inn.

**Battle of the Hofbräuhaus** The first mass meeting of the National Socialist Workers' Party (later the Nazi Party) was held in the Hofbräuhaus in 1920. It soon became regarded as the city's most prestigious political beer-hall arena. Here Hitler established himself as a powerful orator: On 4 November 1921, his storm troops first gained notoriety in a huge brawl, later known as the *Schlacht im Hofbräuhaus* (the Battle of the Hofbräuhaus). Despite the hurling of chairs and beer mugs, Hitler managed to finish his speech.

**World's most famous pub** Undoubtedly the city's best-known institution after the *Oktoberfest*, and a meeting place for visitors from all over the world, the Hofbräuhaus—with its long tables, buxom *Dirndl*-clad waitresses and jolly Bavarian music—is a must for tourists, if only to join in with the popular drinking song '*In München steht ein Hofbräuhaus, eins, zwei, drei, g'soffa*'…(one, two, three and down the hatch).

Top **25**

**22**

## Nationaltheater

**Munich's Nationaltheater ranks among the world's leading opera-houses. One of the few German theatres to have been restored to its magnificent pre-war splendour, it is definitely worth the visit, even if opera is not your scene.**

**People's opera-house** The Nationaltheater has been home to the world famous Bayerische Staatsoper (Bavarian State Opera) since 1818—a distinguished Greek-temple design with a simple colonnaded façade which, after wartime bombing, stood in ruins for years until a group of citizens raised sufficient funds (DM63 million) to restore it to its former glory. It was reopened in 1963.

**Behind the scenes** Most days at 2pm, during a fascinating tour, it is possible to take a rare glimpse backstage and to view the ingenious, high-tech stage machinery. The grandiose auditorium, with five tiers of seating decorated in plush red, gold, ivory and dove blue, is crowned by an enormous chandelier, which magically disappears into the ceiling when the curtain rises. The impressive Greek-style rooms of the foyer provide an elegant setting for the audience to promenade in their finery.

**Opening nights** Many important operas have been premièred here over the centuries, including five by Wagner during the reign of Ludwig II, and many eminent people have conducted, directed and performed here in a repertoire ranging from traditional Munich favourites—Mozart, Wagner and Strauss—to new commissions from living German composers. An opera festival is held here every year in July.

### HIGHLIGHTS

**Outside**
- Façade
- Pediment with Apollo and the Muses, Georg Brenninger, 1972
- Pediment with glass mosaic of *Pegasus with the Horae*, Leo Schwanthaler, 19th century

**Inside**
- Auditorium
- Royal box
- Backstage equipment
- Prompter's box
- Foyer

### INFORMATION

- www.staatsoper.de
- N24; Locator map D3
- Max-Joseph-Platz 2
- 21 85 19 20
- Box office Mon–Fri 10–6, Sat 10–1
- U-or S-Bahn Marienplatz, U-Bahn Odeonsplatz
- 52, 53; tram 19
- Few
- Tour moderate
- Odeonsplatz (➤ 44), Residenz (➤ 45)
- Tickets available in advance at the box office (☎ 21 85 19 20) in Marstallplatz 5, or from the theatre itself one hour before the performance. Guided tours in German (☎ 21 85 10 25) Most days at 2pm, except Aug–end Sep)

Top **25**

**23**

# Deutsches Museum

### HIGHLIGHTS

- Planetarium
- Faraday's Cage and high-voltage demonstration
- First German submarine
- Karl Benz's Automobil Nummer I
- Copy of the 'Puffing Billy' team train
- Reconstruction of a coal mine
- Reconstruction of caves at Lascaux
- Dornier DO 31 and Junkers JU52 aircraft
- 19th-century sailing ship –60m (197ft) long
- Transport Museum

### INFORMATION

**www.deutsches-museum.de**
- O24; Locator map E4
- Museumsinsel 1
- 21 79–1
- Daily 9–5
- Restaurant, railroad-carriage café
- S-Bahn Isartor
- Tram 18
- Excellent
- Expensive

**If you spent one minute at each exhibit, it would take you 36 days to see everything at this museum of superlatives—Munich's most famous, Germany's most visited and one of the world's biggest science museums.**

**Voyage of discovery** In 1903, engineer Oskar von Miller founded the Museum of Masterworks of Science and Technology. After his death, the collection moved to its present building on its own island on the Isar, east of the city. It was officially opened in 1925 and grew over the years to a staggering 17,000-plus exhibits, ranging from the sundial to the space shuttle, with priceless artefacts and historical originals.

**Learning experience** The most popular areas cover mining (including a reconstructed coal mine), computer science and various transportation sections. Alongside original artefacts are audio-visual displays, experiments and hands-on models.

**Unique exhibits** Some of the most dramatic displays are the star shows at the Planetarium (which takes place in the high-tech Forum ➤ 62), an ear-splitting high voltage demonstration that simulates a 220,000-volt flash of lightning, and the vast model railway on the ground level. Other highlights include the first German submarine; one of the first jet aeroplanes; Karl Benz's first car; and the bench on which Otto Hahn proved the splitting of the atom.

Top **25**

**24**

## Englischer Garten

**The English Garden ranks highly on every Münchner's list of favourite city spots. On a sunny day, there's nothing more enjoyable than a walk in this vast, idyllic park where you will see people from all walks of life.**

**Munich's 'green lung'** People come here to enjoy themselves: families boating, musicians busking, children feeding the ducks, New Age groups gathered by the love temple, professionals picnicking in their lunch break, jolly crowds in the packed beer gardens. For this is Munich's beloved 'green lung'—373ha (920 acres) of parkland stretching over 5km (3 miles) along the River Isar, and one of the largest city parks in the world.

**English influences** The English Garden was created by Count Rumford and Ludwig von Sckell in 1789. Breaking away from the French style of manicured lawns and geometrical flowerbeds, they transformed the Wittelsbach hunting ground into an informal, countrified *Volksgarten* (people's park).

**Attractions** Start at the Kleinhesseloher See, an artificial lake with boats for hire. Or spend time relaxing at the Seehaus beer garden before heading south towards the Monopteros, a circular, Greek-style love temple with a splendid view of the park and the distant spires of old Munich. As well as English and Greek influences, the park also has a distinctive oriental flavour with its Japanese Tea House and Chinese Tower. It also marks the city's most famous beer garden—popular for its brass band, old-fashioned children's merry-go-round and permanent *Oktoberfest* atmosphere.

### HIGHLIGHTS

- Chinese Tower
- Kleinhesseloher See and Seehaus
- Monopteros
- Japanese Tea House (tea ceremonies on the second weekend of every month May–end Oct)
- Rumford House

### INFORMATION

- M24–H27; Locator map E1
- Dawn to dusk
- Chinese Tower beer garden, Seehaus restaurant and beer garden, Japanese Tea House, Aumeister restaurant and beer garden (➤ 52)
- U-Bahn Odeonsplatz, Universität, Giselastrasse, Münchener Freiheit
- 44, 53, 54, 154; tram 17
- Rowing boats for hire at the Kleinhesseloher See in summer
- Bayerisches Nationalmuseum (➤ 50), Haus der Kunst (➤ 56)

Top **25**

**25**

# Bayerisches Nationalmuseum

**The Bavarian National Museum is one of Europe's leading museums of folk-art, and is guaranteed to give you a real taste of Bavarian life over the centuries to the present day.**

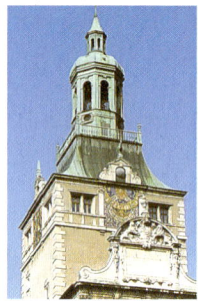

*Top: Riemenschneider woodcarving*

### HIGHLIGHTS

- Medieval model of Munich, Jakob Sandtner
- Augsburg Weaving Room
- Tilman Riemenschneider sculptures
- Crib collection
- Flanders Tapestry Room
- Weaponry Room
- Closet from Palais Tattenbach

### INFORMATION

**www.**bayerisches-nationalmuseum.de
- N25; Locator map F2
- Prinzregentenstrasse 3
- 2 11 24 01
- Tue–Sun 10–5 (Thu until 8pm)
- U-Bahn Lehel
- 53; tram 17
- Good
- Moderate; Sun free
- Englischer Garten (➤ 49)

**Wittelsbach treasures** Thanks to the Wittelsbach rulers' passion for collecting works of art, this museum was founded in 1885 by Maximilian II and transferred to its present site in 1900. Even the building mirrors the various periods represented within the museum in a clever design by Gabriel von Seidl dating from 1900; the west wing is Romanesque, the east wing Renaissance, the tower Baroque and the west end Rococo. The interior is divided into two main collections—Folklore and Art History—providing a comprehensive survey of German cultural history, both sacred and secular, from the early Middle Ages to the present.

**Folklore** A series of rooms authentically decorated with rustic Bavarian furniture, glass, pottery and woodcraft provides a wonderful insight into the country life of bygone years. The Augsburg Room with its outstanding carved ceiling, is particulary attractive. The museum is famous for its sculptures by Hans Leinberger, Ignaz Günther and Tilman Riemenschneider and its large crib collection.

**Art history** This collection consists of a series of specialist departments including Bavarian *Trachten* (traditional costume), tapestries, porcelain, jewellery, armour and the largest ivory collection in Europe. If your interested in how Munich looked 500 years ago, study the medieval model of the city, created by master woodworker Jakob Sandtner.

# MUNICH's
# best

Beer Halls & Beer Gardens  *52–53*

Celebrations  *54*

Lakes  *55*

Museums & Galleries  *56–57*

Castles & Churches  *58–59*

Statues & Fountains  *60*

Modern Architecture  *61*

Attractions for Children  *62*

## Munich's Best

# Beer Halls & Beer Gardens

**In the Top 25**
- 23 CHINESE TOWER (ENGLISCHER GARTEN, ➤ 49)
- 20 HOFBRÄUHAUS (➤ 46)
- 24 SEEHAUS (ENGLISCHER GARTEN, ➤ 49)
- 17 VIKTUALIENMARKT (➤ 43)

**ALTE VILLA (AMMERSEE, ➤ 55)**

**AUGUSTINER-KELLER**
One of Munich's most traditional beer cellars, just a few minutes' walk from the main station. Its popular beer garden seats over 5,000.
✚ N23 ✉ Arnulfstrasse 52 ☎ 59 43 93 🕐 Daily 11.30am–1am 🚇 S-Bahn Hackerbrücke 🚋 Tram 17

**AUMEISTER**
Situated at the northern edge of the English Garden, this former huntsman's lodge makes a perfect place to end a walk along the river.
✚ H26 ✉ Sondermeierstrasse 1 ☎ 32 52 24 🕐 Daily 9am–11pm 🚇 U-Bahn Freimann

**BRÄUSTÜBERL WEIHENSTEPHAN**
This former Benedictine monastery in Freising is said to contain the world's oldest brewery, famous for its *Korbinian* strong beer.
✚ Off map to north ✉ Weihenstephanbrauerei, Freising ☎ (08161) 13004 🕐 Daily 10–11 🚇 S-Bahn Freising

**HACKERKELLER**
Ox-on-the-spit, the house speciality here, is served to the accompaniment of traditional Bavarian music.
✚ 022 ✉ Theresienhöhe 4 ☎ 50 70 04 🕐 10am–midnight 🚇 U-Bahn Theresienwiese

**HIRSCHGARTEN**
Munich's largest beer garden, seating 8,500, is near Schloss Nymphenburg. Children love the deer enclosure and huge park.

### WHAT TO EAT AND DRINK

You can take your own food to most beer gardens. Better still, try some traditional Bavarian *Brotzeit* (snacks, literally 'bread time'): *Radi* (large white radishes), *Brez'n* (pretzel bread), *Obatzda* (Camembert and chive spread), *Steckerlfisch* (smoked mackerel), or *Schweinshax'n* (pork knuckles). Wash it all down with a *Maß* (stein) of beer, or have a *Radler* (mixture of beer and lemonade), or a refreshing *Spezi* (cola and lemonade mix).

*Enjoying a friendly drink in one of Munich's many beer gardens*

# Munich's Best

🏠 M19 ✉ Hirschgartenallee 1 ☎ 17 25 91 🕐 Daily 9am–midnight
🚋 Tram 17

**KLOSTER ANDECHS (AMMERSEE, ➤ 55)**

### LÖWENBRÄUKELLER
During the Lenten 'Strong Beer Season' (➤ 54), men from all over Bavaria visit this beer cellar to pit their strength against each other in a stone-lifting competition.
🏠 M22 ✉ Nymphenburgerstrasse 2 ☎ 52 60 21 🕐 Daily 11am–midnight 🚇 U-Bahn Stiglmaierplatz 🚋 Tram 20, 21

### MAX-EMANUEL-BRÄUEREI
Tiny, crowded beer garden known for its folk music.
🏠 M24 ✉ Adalbertstrasse 33 ☎ 2 71 51 58 🕐 Daily 11–11 (evenings only in winter) 🚇 U-Bahn Universität

### MENTERSCHWAIGE
Royalty used to drink at this ancient beer garden, which today serves excellent Bavarian food in a romantic setting high above the River Isar.
🏠 T22 ✉ Menterschwaigstrasse 4 ☎ 64 07 32 🕐 Daily 11am–midnight 🚋 Tram 15, 25

### AM ROSENGARTEN
Enjoy a hillside view of thousands of roses while sipping your beer in a delightful park setting.
🏠 O20 ✉ Westenstrasse, Westpark ☎ 57 50 53 🕐 Daily 10.30am–11pm 🚇 U-Bahn Westpark 🚌 41, 65; tram 18

### ST. EMMERAMSMÜHLE
Largely populated by the smart set, this is the beer garden in which to see and be seen.
🏠 J27 ✉ St. Emmeram 41 ☎ 95 39 71 🕐 Mon–Sat 11–10, Sun 10am–1am 🚌 37, 88, 188

### TAXISGARTEN
This quiet, shady spot near Schloss Nymphenburg is renowned for its spare ribs.
🏠 L21 ✉ Taxisstrasse 12 ☎ 15 68 27 🕐 Daily 10am–11pm 🚇 U-Bahn Gern

### WALDWIRTSCHAFT GROSSHESSELOHE
A long time local favourite overlooking the Isar gorge and famous for its live jazz.
🏠 Off map to south ✉ Georg-Kalb-Strasse 3 ☎ 74 99 40 30 🕐 Daily 11–11 🚇 S-Bahn Grosshesselohe Isartalbahnhof

### ZUM FLAUCHER
Somewhat off the tourist track, this scenic favourite is next to the River Isar. Families bring their own picnics and candles here in the evening.
🏠 Q22 ✉ Isarauen 1 ☎ 7 23 26 77 🕐 Daily 11–11 (open Sun only in winter) 🚇 U-Bahn Brudermühlstrasse 🚌 Bus 45

*Pub sign in Munich's old town*

### BOCK BEER TEST

Munich is undoubtedly the world's number one beer metropolis. One local speciality is the Strong Bock Beer. At one time a special 'bock test' was used, in the Hofbräuhaus, to check its quality. Fresh May bock beer was poured onto a wooden bench. Hard-headed beer drinkers would sit on this bench for several hours, allowing nature to take its course there and then! If the bench stuck to their backsides when they got up, then the beer was considered good—if not, the beer was too thin.

## Munich's Best

# Celebrations

*Beer tent at the Oktoberfest*

### THE FIRST *OKTOBERFEST*

Amid the heaving throng, the hefty beermaids, the kaleidoscopic fairground and the blast of brass bands in the packed beer-tents, it is easy to forget the origin of the *Oktoberfest*. It all began in 1810 with the wedding party of Crown Prince Ludwig and Princess Theresa—a lavish affair with horse-racing, shooting matches and a fair, but ironically no beer.

### FASCHING

Fasching or Carnival, Munich's 'fifth season', officially starts at 11.11am on 11 November, but celebrations don't really get under way until a few weeks before Lent, when costumed revellers run riot in a dazzling array of carnival processions, street parties and balls, the merriment climaxing in a massive open-air party at the Viktualienmarkt (➤ 43) on Shrove Tuesday.

### STARKBIERZEIT (STRONG BEER SEASON)

In the 17th century, Paulaner monks started to brew a special, nourishing beer with an alcoholic content of 6.7 per cent, which was consumed as 'liquid bread' during Lent. The Pope, not a great beer drinker, pronounced that it was a fitting penance for Lent. The public began to look forward to it each year, and the Strong Beer Festival was born. This unique Munich tradition is best celebrated at the Salvatorkeller am Nockherberg during the three weeks leading up to Easter.

### OKTOBERFEST

The world's biggest beer festival commences on the third Saturday in September when the Lord Mayor taps open the first barrel with the welcome cry '*O'zapft is*' ('It's open') and the massive beer binge begins. Each year around 7 million visitors consume a staggering 6 million litres (over 1 million gallons) of beer, 600,000 chickens and over 400,000 sausages.

### CHRISTKINDLMARKT (CHRISTMAS MARKET)

During Munich's magical Christmas Market, tiny snow-capped wooden huts cluster around Marienplatz, sparkling with light and crammed with Christmas goodies, tree decorations and the beautifully carved cribs that are so famous in Bavaria. After buying your stocking-fillers, gather around the enormous, brightly lit Christmas tree for carols, *Glühwein* and warm gingerbread.

# Munich's Best

# Lakes

> **In the Top 25**
> **20 KLEINHESSELOHER SEE
> (ENGLISCHER GARTEN, ➤ 49)**

### AMMERSEE
Ammersee, with its lake promenades, bustling boat sheds and sandy beaches, is set in lush green countryside at the heart of Munich's lake district, easily reached by S-Bahn. Highlights include a trip on Bavaria's oldest paddle-steamer, the artists' colony at Diessen, live jazz in the Alte Villa beer garden at Utting, and Kloster Andechs, one of Germany's most important pilgrimage destinations, famous worldwide for its centuries-old brewing tradition and its *Andechser Bock* beer.
✚ Off map to southwest  S-Bahn Herrsching

### FELDMOCHINGERSEE
At this beach the water is so clean you could almost drink it. For people with disabilities, there's a machine to raise and lower swimmers into the water.
✚ Off map to north  S-Bahn Feldmoching

### FERINGASEE
One of the most popular lakes near the city, with sandy beaches and good windsurfing.
✚ H29  S-Bahn Unterföhring

### KARLSFELDER SEE
A great place for children, with safe swimming and excellent sports facilities. You might even catch a glimpse of Emil, the local 'Loch Ness' monster.
✚ Off map to northwest  S-Bahn Karlsfeld

### STARNBERGER SEE
The baroque palaces of Bavaria's aristocracy line the banks of the Starnberger See, the largest of the five lakes just south of the city, and the area remains predominantly the domain of the rich and famous. Today, as Munich's main summer playground, it offers horse-riding, golf, swimming and sailing, set against a breathtaking Alpine backdrop.
✚ Off map to southwest
 S-Bahn Starnberg

### MYSTERIOUS PHENOMENA

While the Starnberger See is famed for its supposed sea monster—a giant worm, which agitates the water even when there isn't a breath of wind—the Ammersee offers a curious, inexplicable phenomenon: A *Schaukelwelle* (rocking wave) that crosses the Ammersee from north to south and back again like a giant pendulum every 24 minutes, the water rising and falling about 10cm (4in) against the shore.

*Boats for hire on the Ammersee*

# Munich's Best

# Museums & Galleries

> **In the Top 25**
> 8 **ALTE PINAKOTHEK (► 33)**
> 25 **BAYERISCHES NATIONALMUSEUM (► 50)**
> 3 **BMW-MUSEUM (► 28)**
> 4 **DACHAU MEMORIAL MUSEUM (► 29)**
> 22 **DEUTSCHES MUSEUM (► 48)**
> 6 **LENBACHHAUS (► 31)**
> 12 **MÜNCHNER STADTMUSEUM (► 38)**
> 9 **NEUE PINAKOTHEK (► 34)**
> 1 **NYMPHENBURG PORCELAIN MUSEUM (► 26)**
> 10 **PINAKOTHEK DER MODERNE (► 35)**
> 16 **SPIELZEUGMUSEUM (► 42)**

### VALENTIN'S DAY

Karl Valentin (1882–1948), Bavaria's answer to Charlie Chaplin, was loved for his quirky wit and misanthropic humour. He started out in beer halls but soon attracted the attention of Schwabing intellectuals, including dramatist Bertolt Brecht. Perhaps best remembered for his sketch in which he put fish in a bird-cage and birds in an aquarium, his statue (along with those of other popular folk entertainers) can be seen today at the Viktualienmarkt (► 43).

### ALPINE MUSEUM

Everything you want to know about mountaineering in the Alps from 1760 onwards, plus occasional temporary exhibitions.
➕ N24 ✉ Praterinsel 5 ☎ 2 11 22 40 🕐 Tue–Fri 1–6, Thu, Sat–Sun 11–6 🚇 U- or S-Bahn Isartor 🚋 Tram 17

### ERWIN VON KREIBIG GALLERY

Temporary exhibitions of promising local artists showcase the latest trends in the Munich art scene.
➕ L19 ✉ Südliches Schlossrondell 1, Schloss Nymphenburg ☎ 1 78 11 69 🕐 Tue–Thu, Sat–Sun 2–5 🚋 Tram 12, 17 💰 Inexpensive

### FLUGWERFT SCHLEISSHEIM

A must for aeroplane buffs, this extension of the Deutsches Museum's aviation display is located on a disused airfield.
➕ Off map to north ✉ Effnerstrasse 18 ☎ 3 15 71 40 🕐 Daily 9–5 🚇 S-Bahn Oberschleissheim 🚌 292 💰 Moderate

### GERMAN HUNTING AND FISHING MUSEUM

The most important collection of its kind in Germany, including the Wolpertinger, a 'hoax' animal resembling a marmot with webbed feet, antlers and wings, found only in Bavaria.
➕ N23 ✉ Neuhauser Strasse 2 ☎ 22 05 22 🕐 Daily 9.30–5 (Thu until 8) 🚇 U- or S-Bahn Marienplatz 💰 Moderate

### GERMAN THEATRE MUSEUM

This small but fascinating display of set designs, costumes, photographs and props brings Germany's rich theatrical past to life.
➕ N24 ✉ Galeriestrasse 4a ☎ 2 10 69 10 🕐 Tue, Thu 10–noon, 2–4 🚇 U-Bahn Odeonsplatz 💰 Moderate

### HAUS DE KUNST

This monstrous Nazi building—one of the few that Allied bombardments missed—was nicknamed the '*weisswurst*' (white sausage) gallery by Hitler's opponents, because of its crude

## Munich's Best

neo-classical columns. After seizing power in 1933, Adolf Hitler ordered the construction of a temple of art to house his personal vision of truly German art. This immense, pseudo-classical building, built by Paul Ludwig Troost, was the first monumental Nazi building in Munich, and set the pattern for later designs. Today, its lofty interior provides an impressive forum for major modern art exhibitions.

M24 ✉ Prinzregentenstrasse 1 ☎ 21 12 70 ◉ Daily 10–8 (Thu until 10) U-Bahn Odeonsplatz or Lehel 53; tram 17

### MUSEUM VILLA STUCK

This stunning Jugendstil villa, the former home of Franz von Stuck, has been beautifully restored and contains changing exhibitions dedicated to 20th-century art.

N25 ✉ Prinzregentenstrasse 60 ☎ 45 55 51 25 ◉ Wed–Sun 11–6 53; tram 18 U-Bahn Prinzregentenplatz ✋ Inexpensive

### SCHACK-GALERIE

This intimate gallery captures the artistic spirit of 19th-century German art.

N25 ✉ Prinzregentenstrasse 9 ☎ 23 80 52 24 ◉ Wed–Sun 10–5 53; tram 18 U-Bahn Lehel ✋ Inexpensive

### VALENTIN-MUSEUM

Showcase for the eccentric humour of Munich's Karl Valentin, with oddities like his first snow sculpture 'now unfortunately melted'. Bizarre opening times too.

N24 ✉ Tal 50 ☎ 22 32 66 ◉ Mon, Tue, Fri, Sat 11.01–5.29, Sun 10.01–5.29 S-Bahn Isartor ✋ Free

### ZAM (CENTRE FOR EXTRAORDINARY MUSEUMS)

Munich's most-unusual collections—chamber pots, pedal cars, padlocks and even Easter bunnies.

N24 ✉ Westen-riederstrasse 41 ☎ 2 90 41 21 ◉ Daily 10–6 S-Bahn Isartor ✋ Moderate

### CITY OF ART

Munich claims to be one of the richest European cities of art, thanks largely to the Wittelsbach family, the ambitious rulers of Munich who avidly collected priceless works of art for over 650 years. The majority of the hundred or so museums and galleries in town offer free entrance on Sundays and the Tourist Office produces a useful Official Monthly Programme of Events with up-to-date information on current exhibitions.

*Above: Der Olymp, by Jenssens, New Picture Gallery*

*Right: Foyer of the Schack-Galerie*

**Munich's** Best

# Castles & Churches

### LOVERS' RENDEZVOUS

The undeniably romantic castle Schloss Blutenberg (above) was originally built as a love-nest for Agnes Bernauer by her secret lover Duke Albrecht III in 1438. Sadly, their romance never had a chance to flourish as, shortly after completion of the magical castle, she was accused of being a witch and was drowned in the Danube at Straubing.

#### In the Top 25
- **ASAMKIRCHE (➤ 37)**
- **FRAUENKIRCHE (➤ 39)**
- **PETERSKIRCHE (➤ 41)**
- **RESIDENZ (➤ 45)**
- **SCHLEISSHEIM PALACES (➤ 30)**
- **SCHLOSS NYMPHENBURG (➤ 26)**

### ASAM-SCHLÖSSL MARIA EINSIEDEL
This once ordinary house was transformed into a royal country residence in the early 18th century, with a magnificent façade painted by Cosmas Damian Asam. Today it is a restaurant.
✚ R21　✉ Benediktbeurer Strasse 19　☎ 7 23 63 73
🕒 Restaurant daily 11am–1am　Ⓤ U-Bahn Thalkirchen

### DAMENSTIFTSKIRCHE ST. ANNA
Only the ornate façade of St. Anne's survived World War II; the church was rebuilt in the 1950s. The interior, decorated in pastel shades, contains stucco work and frescoes by the Asam brothers.
✚ N23　✉ Damenstiftstrasse 1　Ⓤ U- or S-Bahn Karlsplatz

### DREIFALTIGKEITSKIRCHE
The Church of the Holy Trinity was built in the early 18th century following the prophecies of a young Munich mystic who claimed that Divine Judgement was about to strike and the city could be saved only if an oath was taken to build a church. Curiously, it was one of the few churches undamaged during World War II.
✚ N23　✉ Pacellistrasse 6　Ⓤ U- or S-Bahn Karlsplatz

### HEILIGGEISTKIRCHE
The Gothic Church of the Holy Ghost, at the northern end of the Viktualienmarkt, is crammed with religious treasures.
✚ N24　✉ Tal 77　Ⓤ U- or S-Bahn Marienplatz

# Munich's Best

### LUDWIGSKIRCHE
Peter Cornelius's *Last Judgement*, the fresco in this elegant church, is the world's largest after Michelangelo's *Last Judgement* in the Sistine Chapel. It took four years to complete.
🚇 M24  ✉ Ludwigstrasse 20  Ⓤ U-Bahn Universität

### SCHLOSS BLUTENBURG
An idyllic moated 15th-century castle in Obermenzing. This one-time Wittelsbach summer residence has a chapel full of treasures. It also contains an international collection of children's books—the largest library of youth literature in the world, with over 500,000 books in some 100 different languages.
🚇 L16  ✉ Seldweg 15, Obermenzing  ☎ 8 91 21 10  Ⓒ Chapel daily Apr–end Sep 9–5; Oct–end Mar 10–4. Library Mon–Fri 2pm–6pm  Ⓢ S-Bahn Obermenzing  💶 Free admission to chapel

### SCHLOSS DACHAU
Only one wing remains of this popular 16th-century summer residence and hunting ground for Munich royals. It now contains a folk museum and a café that serves the best pastries in Munich.
🚇 Off map to northwest  ☎ (08131) 87923  Ⓒ Apr–end Sep Tue–Sun 9–6; Oct–end Mar 10–4  🍴 Café on premises  Ⓢ S-Bahn Dachau  💶 Inexpensive

### SCHLOSS FÜRSTENRIED
This baroque castle, scene of King Maximilian II's magnificent hunting parties, is aligned with the Frauenkirche 13km (8 miles) away. The wonderful view down the avenue of lime trees is interupted by a motorway.
🚇 S18  ✉ Forst-Kasten-Allee  Ⓤ U-Bahn Basler Strasse

### SCHLOSS SURESNES
After the collapse of the socialist republic in 1919, this 18th-century summer residence served as a hideaway for the writer and revolutionary Ernst Toller until his arrest here. It then became home to artist Paul Klee until 1921.
🚇 L24  ✉ Werneckstrasse 24  Ⓤ U-Bahn Münchener Freiheit

### THEATINERKIRCHE
Considered by many to be the most beautiful church in Munich, with its brilliant yellow façade (the first example of Bavarian baroque) the Theatinerkirche became an important architectural model for later Bavarian churches.
🚇 N24  ✉ Theatinerstrasse 22  Ⓤ U-Bahn Odeonsplatz

### A BIRTHDAY CHURCH
The Court Church of St. Kajetan was originally built to celebrate the birth of a son and heir to Princess Henriette Adelaide and Elector Ferdinand Maria, and their joy is mirrored in the exuberant interior ornamentation, modelled on San Andrea del Valle in Rome. The church was assigned to the monks of the Theatine order, hence the name Theatinerkirche.

*The Theatinerkirche*

# Munich's Best

# Statues & Fountains

## A FULL PURSE

There was once a fish market next to Konrad Knoll's famous Fish Fountain (1865) in Marienplatz. It then became the scene of the traditional 'Butcher's Leap', where butchers' apprentices were 'baptized' into the profession. Today, they say that if you wash your purse here on Ash Wednesday, it will never be empty. To this day, the Lord Mayor washes the City Purse here every year.

*The Brunnenbuberl*

### In the Top 25
**18 BRUNNENHOF FOUNTAIN (RESIDENZ, ➤ 45)**

### ANGEL OF PEACE
This gleaming golden figure, perched high above the River Isar, was built for the 25th anniversary of Germany's victory over France in 1871.
✚ N25 ✉ Prinzregentenstrasse 🚌 53

### BRUNNENBUBERL (FOUNTAIN BOY)
Even after public outcry greeted this naked young boy in 1895, sculptor Mathias Gastiner refused to supply a fig leaf.
✚ N23 ✉ Neuhauser Strasse Ⓤ U- or S-Bahn Karlsplatz

### CATTLE MARKET FOUNTAIN
Three cows mark this ancient marketplace, today a popular picnic spot.
✚ N23 ✉ Rindermarkt Ⓤ U- or S-Bahn Marienplatz

### MARIENSÄULE
Marienplatz owes its name to this gracious figure of the Virgin Mary. All distances in Bavaria are measured from this point.
✚ N23 ✉ Marienplatz Ⓤ U- or S-Bahn Marienplatz

### MONUMENT TO MAX-JOSEPH IV
Max Joseph, the first Wittelsbach king, wanted a more dignified standing pose but died before the statue was finished. His son, Ludwig I, settled for this seated version.
✚ N24 ✉ Max-Joseph-Platz Ⓤ U- or S-Bahn Marienplatz

### PUMUCKL FOUNTAIN
This cheeky character douses passers-by when they least expect it.
✚ K23 ✉ Luitpold Park Ⓤ U-Bahn Scheidplatz

### STATUE OF BAVARIA
This famous lady representing Bavaria is 18m (60ft) high. Climb the 112 steps inside to the top for a splendid view from.
✚ O22 ✉ Theresienwiese Ⓤ U-Bahn Theresienwiese

### WALKING MAN
This wacky, 1995 sculpture by American sculptor Jonathan Borofsky is five storeys (17m/56ft) tall.
✚ M24 ✉ Leopoldstrasse 36 Ⓤ U-Bahn Giselastrasse

### WITTELSBACH FOUNTAIN
The two figures of Munich's loveliest neo-classical fountain (1895) symbolize the destructive and healing power of water.
✚ N23 ✉ Lenbachplatz Ⓤ U- or S-Bahn Karlsplatz

# Munich's Best

# Modern Architecture

**In the Top 25**
- **NEUE PINAKOTHEK (► 34)**
- **OLYMPIAPARK (► 27)**

### BAVARIAN STATE CHANCELLERY
The gleaming glass and steel Staatskanzlei building is framed by a Renaissance-style arcade and has the dome of the former Army Museum as its centrepiece.
✚ N24 ✉ Hofgarten Ⓢ U-Bahn Odeonsplatz

### BMW HEADQUARTERS
This giant, silver, four-cylinder building resembles a four-leaf clover. It was built between 1970 and 1972 by Viennese architect Karl Schwanzer to signal the company's technical orientation.
✚ J23 ✉ Petuelring 130 Ⓢ U-Bahn Petuelring

### HAUS DER KUNST (► 56)

### JUGENDSTILHAUS AINMILLERSTRASSE
Munich's first Jugendstil house (1900) has been restored to its original glory.
✚ L24 ✉ Ainmillerstrasse 22 Ⓢ U-Bahn Giselastrasse

### KULTURZENTRUM GASTEIG
This striking combination of red brick and glass contains a high-tech concert hall, conservatory and municipal library.
✚ O25 ✉ Rosenheimerstrasse Ⓢ S-Bahn Rosenheimerplatz

### MÜLLERSCHES VOLKSBAD (► 85)

### MUNICH AIRPORT
Displays of light, space and movement counterbalance the more functional aspects of this state-of-the-art complex.
✚ Off map to northeast ✉ Flughafen Ⓢ S-Bahn Flughafen

### MUSIKHOCHSCHULE
Designed on Hitler's instruction by Paul Ludwig Troost, the music academy (formerly Hitler's 'Temple of Honour') is connected to the Haus der Kulturinstitute opposite by an enormous underground bunker system.
✚ M23 ✉ Arcisstrasse 12 Ⓢ U-Bahn Königsplatz

### POST-UND-WOHNGEBÄUDE
One of Germany's most important buildings from the 1920s, this post office-cum-apartment block has an unusual, elegantly curved façade.
✚ O22 ✉ Goetheplatz 1 Ⓢ U-Bahn Goetheplatz

### HYPO TOWERS

The post-war city contains a remarkable number of modern architectural gems. One of its most original wonders—the 114-m (375-ft) Hypobank headquarters (✉ Arabellastrasse 12 Ⓢ U-Bahn Arabellapark)—pierces the skyline in a striking series of shimmering glass and aluminium prisms, each of a different height and size. It was described by designers Walther and Bea Bentz as 'white sails billowing between silver masts'.

61

# Munich's Best

## Attractions for Children

---

**In the Top 25**
- **3 BMW-MUSEUM (➤ 28)**
- **22 DEUTSCHES MUSEUM (➤ 48)**
- **24 ENGLISCHER GARTEN (➤ 49)**
- **12 MÜNCHNER STADTMUSEUM (➤ 38)**
- **10 SPIELZEUGMUSEUM (➤ 42)**

---

### MUNICH'S VERY OWN HOLLYWOOD

Children will love directing and starring in their own films, watching stuntmen in action and exploring familiar sets (including an entire Berlin street) at the Bavaria Film Studios, location for many famous films including *Enemy Mine* and *The Never-Ending Story*. Munich has always had strong ties to the film industry, and has a Film Museum (➤ 38), a summer Film Festival, a European Film College and a staggering 82 cinemas (➤ 79).

### BAVARIA FILM TOUR
Glimpse behind the scenes of Europe's largest film studios, and learn the tricks of the trade.
🔳 Off map to south ✉ Bavariafilmplatz ☎ 64 99 20 00 🕐 Daily 9–4 (3 in winter) 🚋 Tram 25 💰 Expensive

### BAVARIAN OBSERVATORY
A late-night treat for kids; staff will help find specific stars and comets, and there's a planetarium.
🔳 P25 ✉ Rosenheimerstrasse 145 ☎ 40 62 39 🕐 Sep–end Mar Mon–Fri at 8pm (9pm rest of year) 🚇 U-Bahn Karl-Preis-Platz 💰 Moderate

### CHILDREN'S THEATRES (➤ 82, 83)

### CIRCUS KRONE
Munich's internationally acclaimed circus offers dazzling performances in its permanent big top from December to March.
🔳 M22 ✉ Marsstrasse 43 ☎ 5 45 80 00 🕐 Telephone for times 🚉 S-Bahn Hackerbrücke

### FILM MUSEUM (➤ 38)

### FORUM AM DEUTSCHES MUSEUM
A high-tech entertainment complex containing Germany's first IMAX cinema (➤ 79) and the world's most modern planetarium.
🔳 O24 ✉ Museumsinsel 1 ☎ 2 11 25–0 🕐 Daily 9am–11pm 🚉 S-Bahn Isartor 💰 Expensive

### HELLABRUNN ZOO
The world's first 'Geo-Zoo' with animals grouped according to their regions of origin.
🔳 R22 ✉ Tierparkstrasse 30 ☎ 62 50 80 🕐 Apr–end Sep daily 8–6; Oct–end Mar daily 9–5 🚇 U-Bahn Thalkirchen 🚌 52 💰 Expensive

*Steiff Teddy Bear (1907), Toy Museum*

### INTERNATIONAL YOUTH LIBRARY (➤ 59)

### MUSEUM MENSCH UND NATUR
Hands-on displays at the 'Museum of Man and Nature' show man's relationship with the natural world in an educational but fun way.
🔳 L19 ✉ Schloss Nymphenburg ☎ 1 79 58 91 20 🕐 Tue–Sun 9–5; closed public hols 🚌 41; tram 12, 17 💰 Inexpensive

# MUNICH
## where to...

**EAT**
Best in Town  64
Bavarian Restaurants  65
International Cuisine  66–67
Vegetarian Restaurants  68
Breakfast Cafés  69
Tea, Coffee &
    Ice-Cream Cafés  70
Snacks  71

**SHOP**
Antiques, Design & Books  72
Gifts & Bavarian Souvenirs  73
Department Stores, Food
    Stores & Markets  74–75
Specialist Shops  76–77
Fashion Shops  78

**BE ENTERTAINED**
Cinemas & Nightclubs  79
Bars, Cafés & Live Music  80–81
Theatre, Classical Music,
    Opera & Ballet  82–83
Sport & Activities  84–85

**STAY**
Luxury Hotels  86
Mid-Range Hotels  87
Budget Accommodation  88

# Where to Eat

# Best in Town

## PRICES

Expect to pay per person for a meal, excluding drink:

€ up to €20

€€ €20–40

€€€ over €40

## DINING OUT

Eating and drinking in Bavaria, and especially in Munich, are major pastimes, with restaurants ranging from the culinary delights of Tantris and other gastronomic temples famous throughout Germany to market snack-stalls known as *Imbiss*. Generally speaking, eating out is not cheap, and you need to reserve a table in most places. Restaurants and cafés listed here, like most around town, are open all day unless otherwise stated. Service is usually included in the price, although a small tip is welcomed.

### BOGENHAUSER HOF (€€€)

This small countrified restaurant is located in a picture-book house, which stands in a pretty garden. Reservations are essential if you wish to sample the inspired French-style cuisine and attentive service, as its close proximity to the Maximilaneum makes it a popular haunt for members of Parliament.
M25 ✉ Ismaningerstrasse 85 ☎ 98 55 86 ⓘ Closed Sun 🚋 Tram 18

### GLOCKENBACH (€€€)

Dine in style amid wood-panelled walls hung with modern art at this esteemed restaurant. The food is top-class with no unnecessary frills.
024 ✉ Kapuzinerstrasse 29 ☎ 59 90 87 87 ⓘ Tue–Sat 🚇 U-Bahn Goetheplatz

### HALALI (€€€)

The secret of Halali's success is its old Bavarian style and good, unpretentious, regional home cooking. Try the tender venison in a juniper berry sauce with cranberries and wild mushrooms.
M24 ✉ Schönfeldstrasse 22 ☎ 28 59 09 ⓘ Mon–Fri lunch, dinner, Sat dinner only 🚇 U-Bahn Odeonsplatz

### KÄFER-SCHÄNKE (€€€)

This warren of rooms above the famous Käfer delicatessen promises a gastronomic experience with creative dishes and a lavish buffet. Worth the expense.
N25 ✉ Prinzregentenstrasse 73 ☎ 41 68-0 ⓘ Mon–Sat noon–midnight 🚇 U-Bahn Prinzregentenplatz

### KÖNIGSHOF (€€€)

This gastronomic temple, in one of Munich's finest hotels, offers tempting regional delicacies and an extensive wine list in an elegant setting overlooking Karlsplatz.
N23 ✉ Karlsplatz 25 ☎ 55 13 60 ⓘ Tue–Sat lunch, dinner 🚇 U- or S-Bahn Karlsplatz

### MASSIMILIANO (€€€)

Italian influenced haute cuisine produced with flair and imagination. Excellent wine list and al fresco dining in summer.
024/025 ✉ Rablstrasse 10 ☎ 4 48 44 77 ⓘ Lunch, dinner 🚇 S-Bahn Rosenheimer Platz

### SCHUHBECK'S IN DEN SÜDTIROLER STUBEN (€€€)

In this Michelin-starred restaurant, chef Alfons Schuhbeck prides himself on his modern, light interpretation of traditional Bavarian cuisine, using the best in local, seasonal produce.
N24 ✉ Platzl 6–8 ☎ 21 66 90-0 ⓘ Mon 6pm–11pm, Tue–Sat noon–2.30, 6–11 🚇 S-Bahn Marienplatz

### TANTRIS (€€€)

Munich's top restaurant, renamed under the guidance of top chef Hans Haas, for its excellent service and contemporary cuisine.
K24 ✉ Johann-Fichte-Strasse 7 ☎ 36 19 59-0 ⓘ Tue–Sat lunch, dinner 🚇 U-Bahn Dietlindenstrasse

# Where to Eat

# Bavarian Restaurants

### AUGUSTINER GASTSTÄTTEN (€€)
Munich's oldest still-standing brewery, now a popular inn, serves reasonably priced Bavarian fare. Beer was brewed here until 1897.
➕ N23 ✉ Neuhauser Strasse 27 ☎ 23 18 32 57 🚇 U- or S-Bahn Karlsplatz

### GEORGENHOF (€€)
Relax and enjoy game specialities and delicious apple strudel in this cosy, rustic restaurant, lit by candles and an open fire.
➕ L24 ✉ Friedrichstrasse 1 ☎ 39 31 01 🕐 Daily noon–11pm 🚇 U-Bahn Giselastrasse

### HAXENBAUER (€€)
Watch the cooks turning giant shanks of pork (*Schweinshax'n*) over open beechwood fires in this ancient inn. Huge, hearty portions for meat lovers.
➕ N24 ✉ Sparkassenstrasse ☎ 29 66 54-0 🕐 Daily 11am–midnight 🚇 U- or S-Bahn Marienplatz

### HUNDSKUGEL (€€)
Wind the clock back to the Middle Ages at Munich's oldest inn, dating from 1440.
➕ N23 ✉ Hotterstrasse 18 ☎ 26 42 72 🕐 Daily 10.30am–midnight 🚇 U- or S-Bahn Marienplatz

### ISARBRÄU (€€)
This converted railway station brews its own *Weissbier* and has an unusual menu of beer-inspired cuisine .
➕ Off map to south ✉ Kreuzeckstrasse 23 ☎ 79 89 61 🕐 Daily 10am–midnight 🚇 S-Bahn Grosshesselohe

### NÜRNBERGER BRATWURSTGLÖCKL (€)
An ancient tavern, best known for its *Nürnberger Bratwurst* (sausages from Nuremberg), grilled over an open beechwood fire and served on a bed of *sauerkraut*.
➕ N23 ✉ Frauenplatz 9 ☎ 22 03 85 🕐 Mon–Sat 10am–midnight 🚇 U- or S-Bahn Marienplatz

### RATSKELLER (€€)
Good solid cuisine under the vaulted arches of the New Town Hall's cellar.
➕ N23 ✉ Marienplatz 8 ☎ 21 99 89-0 🕐 Daily 10am–midnight 🚇 U- or S-Bahn Marienplatz

### SPATENHAUS (€€)
Opposite the opera and popular with the after-theatre crowd with a pleasant atmosphere and an excellent menu.
➕ N24 ✉ Residenzstrasse 12 ☎ 2 90 70 60 🕐 Daily 11.30am–12.30am 🚇 U- or S-Bahn Marienplatz

### WEISSES BRÄUHAUS (€)
The *Weisswürste* here are easily the best in town, accompanied by a wickedly strong *Weissbier*.
➕ N24 ✉ Tal 7 ☎ 29 01 38-0 🕐 Daily 9am–11.30pm 🚇 U- or S-Bahn Marienplatz

### ZUR SCHWAIGE (€€)
Nourishing traditonal fare in the south wing of Schloss Nymphenburg (▶ 26), or in the garden.
➕ L19 ✉ Schloss Nymphenburg ☎ 17 44 21 🕐 Daily 11.30am–11pm 🚇 Tram 17

---

### RUSTIC ATMOSPHERE

Wooden tables covered with blue-and-white chequered tablecloths, benches and carved chairs lend a cosy feel to a typical Bavarian restaurant. Murals depicting mountains, lakes and hunting scenes are hung on the walls next to prized antlers or a collection of beer mugs. Try the hearty *Schweinebraten* (roast pork) with *Sauerkraut* and *Knödel* (dumplings) while you soak up the atmosphere.

### SAUSAGES

Sausages of every shape, size and colour are undoubtedly the hallmark of the Bavarian diet. The famous Munich *Weisswürste* (white veal sausages flecked with parsley) are served in a tureen of hot water, peeled before eating and smothered in sweet mustard. Tradition has it that a white sausage mustn't hear the chimes of midday, so everyone crowds the restaurants at 11am to enjoy this local delicacy. *Guten Appetit!*

## Where to Eat

# International Cuisine

### FOREIGN INFLUENCES

With one out of five people living in Munich carrying a foreign passport, it is understandable that an impressive array of international specialities is served in the city's 6,000 restaurants. Health-conscious diners have lately been enticed by Asian food, especially Japanese, which is deemed lighter than traditional Bavarian fare, while French and Italian cuisine continues to dominate at the top-flight restaurants in the city.

### ACQUARELLO (€€€)
The finest Italian restaurant in town, with one Michelin star, delicate, subtly composed cuisine and an impressive wine list.
N26 ✉ Mühlbauerstrasse 36 ☎ 4 70 48 48 ⏰ Mon–Fri noon–2.30, 6.30–11, Sat–Sun 6.30–10.30 🚇 U-Bahn Böhmerwaldplatz

### AUSTERNKELLER (€€)
Munich's best address for seafood specialities.
N24 ✉ Stollbergstrasse 11 ☎ 29 87 87 ⏰ Daily 5pm–11.30pm 🚋 Tram 19

### BENJARONG (€€€)
One of Germany's top Thai restaurants, with prices to match, but worth it.
N24 ✉ Falckenbergstrasse 7 ☎ 2 91 30 55 ⏰ Lunch, dinner; closed Sun 🚋 Tram 19

### BISTRO TERRINE (€€€)
Exquisite French food in a smart art deco setting.
M24 ✉ Amalienstrasse 89 ☎ 28 17 80 ⏰ Tue–Fri lunch, Mon–Sat dinner 🚇 U-Bahn Universität

### CAFÉ GLOCKENSPIEL (€€€)
One of Munich's most romantic settings directly opposite the famous Glockenspiel. There's also a popular café and bar.
N24 ✉ Marienplatz 28 ☎ 26 42 56 ⏰ Restaurant daily 10–1, 7–1am. Café daily 10am–1am 🚇 U- or S-Bahn Marienplatz

### CHAO PRAYA (€€)
Reserve in advance for this popular Thai restaurant.
M21 ✉ Nymphenburger Strasse 128 ☎ 1 29 31 90 ⏰ Lunch, dinner; closed Sat lunch 🚇 U-Bahn Rotkreuzplatz

### DREIGROSCHENKELLER (€€)
Cellar restaurant dedicated to the famous 'Threepenny Opera' by Bertold Brecht and Kurt Weill. Mon–Thu at 10pm, its hearty food and home-brewed beer is accompanied by drama students performing songs from the opera.
O24 ✉ Lilienstrasse 2 ☎ 48 90 29-0 🚋 52, 56; tram 18

### GEISEL'S VINOTHEK (€€)
A small, candlelit restaurant with a rustic ambiance, an impressive wine list and a satisfying menu of French, Italian and German delicacies.
N23 ✉ Schützenstrasse 11 ☎ 55 13 71 40 ⏰ Daily 11am–1am 🚇 U- or S-Bahn Hauptbahnhof

### GRISSINI (€€)
An excellent Italian restaurant, decorated like an Italian palazzo.
K25 ✉ Helmtrudenstrasse 1 ☎ 36 10 12 13 ⏰ Lunch, dinner; closed Sat lunch 🚇 U-Bahn Dietlindenstrasse

### JOE PEÑA'S (€€)
This Mexican restaurant is always packed due its delicious *fajitas*, *burritos* and *tequilas*.
O24 ✉ Buttermelcherstrasse 17 ☎ 22 64 63 ⏰ Dinner only 🚋 Tram 18

### LA STELLA (€€)
Terrific pizzas draw a young crowd to this

# Where to Eat

excellent trattoria.
🟦 L24 ✉ Hohenstaufenstrasse 2 ☎ 34 17 79 🕐 Lunch, dinner 🚇 U-Bahn Giselastrasse

### LE CEZANNE (€€€)
This tiny bistro specializes in Provençal fare.
🟦 L24 ✉ Konradstrasse 1 ☎ 39 18 05 🕐 Tue–Sun evenings only 🚇 U-Bahn Giselastrasse

### LENBACH (€€€)
Sir Terence Conran designed this restaurant, one of the most sophisticated in town, on the theme of the Seven Sins.
🟦 N23 ✉ Ottostrasse 6 ☎ 54 91 30-0 🕐 Lunch, dinner; closed Sun 🚇 U- or S-Bahn Karlsplatz

### MAREDO (€€)
The best steak and salad in town is only a stone's throw from Marienplatz.
🟦 N24 ✉ Tal 8 ☎ 29 46 61 🕐 Daily 11.30am–11.30pm 🚇 U- or S-Bahn Marienplatz

### OSTERIA (€€€)
Upmarket Italian cuisine in beautiful surroundings in this historic restaurant.
🟦 M23 ✉ Schellingstrasse 62 ☎ 2 72 03 07 🕐 Closed Sun 🚌 53

### PAPATAKIS (€€)
This Greek restaurant is the place to be at weekends if plate-throwing and dancing on the table is your scene.
🟦 L24 ✉ Leopoldstrasse 43 ☎ 34 13 05 🕐 Lunch, dinner 🚌 33

### RUE DES HALLES (€€€)
Sophisticated, Parisian dining in fashionable Haidhausen.
🟦 O25 ✉ Steinstrasse 18 ☎ 48 56 75 🕐 Dinner only 🚇 S-Bahn Rosenheimer Platz

### SEOUL (€€)
Munich's only Korean resataurant is in the heart of Schwabing.
🟦 K24 ✉ Leopoldstrasse 122 ☎ 34 81 04 🕐 Lunch, dinner; closed 1st, 3rd Mon of month 🚇 U-Bahn Münchener Freiheit

### SHOYA (€€)
Authentic, yet realistically priced Japanese restaurant.
🟦 M23 ✉ Gabelsbergerstrasse 85 ☎ 5 23 62 49 🕐 Dinner only 🚇 U-Bahn Theresienstrasse

### TRADER VIC'S (€€€)
A varied Polynesian menu ranging from Wanton soup to barbecued spare ribs or Calcutta lobster. Excellent cocktails.
🟦 N23 ✉ Hotel Bayerischer Hof, Promenadeplatz 6 ☎ 22 61 92 🕐 Daily 5pm–3am 🚇 U- or S-Bahn Marienplatz

### TRESZNJEWSKI (€€)
This trendy brasserie, opposite the Neue Pinakothek (▶ 34), is packed from breakfast until the early hours.
🟦 M23 ✉ Theresienstrasse 72 ☎ 28 23 49 🕐 Daily 8am–3am 🚋 Tram 27

### VINAIOLO (€€)
This top notch Italian restaurant, located in fashionable Haidhausen, is reasonably priced.
🟦 O25 ✉ Steinstrasse 42 ☎ 48 95 03 56 🕐 Tue–Sun noon–2, 6.30–1, Mon 6.30–1 🚇 S-Bahn Rosenheimer Platz 🚋 Tram 15, 19, 25

---

### 'MAHLZEIT!'

*Mahlzeiten* (mealtimes) are comparatively early in Munich, because most people start work early (around 7–8am). Lunch is eaten between 11.30 and 2 and is for many the main meal of the day, followed by a light supper or *Abendbrot* ('evening bread'). Restaurants usually serve dinner between 6.30 and 11pm when it is polite to wish fellow diners *'Guten Appetit'*. However, during the day it is more common to hear the word *'Mahlzeit'*.

# Where to Eat

# Vegetarian Restaurants

## VEGETARIAN SURPRISE

Think of Bavarian cuisine and many people conjure up images of enormous joints of meat and miles of sausages. However, Munich offers some excellent vegetarian restaurants. Their menus are particularly interesting during *Spargelzeit* (Asparagus Season) in May and June when asparagus is served in an amazing variety of ways.

### BASIC BISTRO (€–€€)
Popular with vegetarians and vegans alike for its delicious international cuisine ranging from Italian antipasti and Lebanese *tabouleh* to Asian stir-fries and salads. Try the house speciality—American-style smoothies.
✚ L23 ✉ Schleißheimer Strasse 162 ☎ 32 38 47 26 ⏰ Mon–Fri 9–8, Sat 9–6 Ⓤ U-Bahn Hohenzollernplatz 🚋 Tram 12, 27

### BON VALEUR (€)
This simple, friendly café offers delicious meat-free panini, unusual salad combinations, homemade cakes and freshly squeezed juices.
✚ N23 ✉ Sonnenstrasse 17 ☎ 54 88 39 94 ⏰ Mon–Thu 10–10, Fri–Sat 10am–1am, Sun noon–8; closed Sat evening and Sun Jul–Sep Ⓤ U- and S-Bahn Karlsplatz, U-Bahn Sendlinger Tor

### BUXS (€)
You pay by the weight of your plate in this cafeteria-style restaurant, which serves an impressive array of hot and cold dishes.
✚ N24 ✉ Frauenstrasse 9 ☎ 2 91 95 50 ⏰ Mon–Fri 11–6.45, Sat 11–3pm Ⓤ S-Bahn Isartor

### CAFÉ IGNAZ (€)
One of Munich's few non-smoking cafés, serving some of the best vegetarian pizzas and risotto in town.
✚ L23 ✉ Georgenstrasse 67 ☎ 271 60 93 ⏰ Mon–Fri 8am–11pm, Sat–Sun 9am–11pm Ⓤ U-Bahn Josephsplatz

### CAFÉ RUFFINI (€)
The vegetarian menu served here is outstanding and the occasional meat dishes are equally good.
✚ L21 ✉ Orffstrasse 22 ☎ 16 11 60 ⏰ Tue–Sun 10am–midnight Ⓤ U-Bahn Rotkreuzplatz

### GOURMET'S GARDEN (€)
This small vegetarian delicatessen in Schwabing specializes in organic cuisine.
✚ L23 ✉ Belgradstrasse 9 ☎ 3 08 84 93 ⏰ Mon–Fri 10–7 Ⓤ 33; tram 12, 27

### MÜNCHNER KARTOFFELHAUS (€)
While not strictly vegetarian, the Munich Potato House offers several delicious meat-free potato dishes.
✚ N24 ✉ Hochbrückenstrasse 3 ☎ 29 63 31 ⏰ Mon–Thu noon–11, Fri–Sat noon–midnight, Sun 5.30–11 Ⓤ U- or S-Bahn Marienplatz and Isartor

### ÖQ HERMANNSDORFER (€)
A small but popular haunt, behind a health-food shop, serving inexpensive vegetarian delicacies and desserts.
✚ N24 ✉ Frauenstrasse 6 ☎ 26 35 25 ⏰ Mon–Fri 9–6 Ⓤ S-Bahn Isartor

### PRINZ MYSHKIN (€€)
Popular, trendy café with a lengthy menu of creative dishes. Don't miss the tofu stroganoff or the *invlotine*, roulades filled with nuts and tofu.
✚ N23 ✉ Hackenstrasse 2 ☎ 26 55 96 ⏰ Daily 11.30am–11.30pm Ⓤ U- or S-Bahn Marienplatz

# Where to Eat

# Breakfast Cafés

**CAFÉ ALTSCHWABING**
Enjoy a leisurely breakfast in this elegant café with tasteful Jugendstil decor.
🛇 M23 ✉ Schellingstrasse 56 ☎ 2 73 10 22 🚇 53; tram 27

**CAFÉ HAIDHAUSEN**
Look out for the 'Hangover' breakfast or try the romantic 'Romeo and Juliet' breakfast for two, served until 4pm.
🛇 O25 ✉ Rosenheimerplatz 4 ☎ 6 88 60 43 🚇 S-Bahn Rosenheimer Platz

**CAFÉ IM HINTERHOF**
Fourteen different breakfast choices from fresh fruit to *weisswürste* in a delightful Jugendstil café.
🛇 O25 ✉ Sedanstrasse 29 ☎ 4 48 99 64 🕙 Mon–Sat 8–8, Sun 9–8 🚇 U- and S-Bahn Ostbahnhof

**CAFÉ SCHWABING**
Bavarian, French and Swiss breakfasts are the speciality of this trendy café. Excellent coffee.
🛇 L23 ✉ Rosenheimerplatz ☎ 3 08 88 56 🚇 33; tram 12

**CAFÉ WIENER PLATZ**
A chic crowd frequents this modern coffee-house with its extensive breakfast menu.
🛇 N25 ✉ Innere-Wiener-Strasse 48 ☎ 4 48 94 94 🚇 Tram 19

**EISBACH**
A chic, modern bar with delicious eggs benedict, bagels, pastries, pancakes and freshly squeezed juices served alfresco in summer.
🛇 N24 ✉ Marstallplatz 3 ☎ 22 80 16 80 🕙 Daily 10am–1am 🚇 Tram 19

**KOSTBAR**
This popular 1970s style café offers a hearty all-day breakfast menu.
🛇 M23 ✉ Augustenstrasse 7 ☎ 54 54 77 99 🕙 Mon–Fri 9am–midnight, Sat 10–6 🚇 U- or S-Bahn Hauptbahnhof 🚇 Tram 20, 21

**MANGOSTIN**
The huge Asian all-you-can eat breakfast buffet here on Sundays is a real treat. Three restaurants (Japanese, Thai and Colonial style) combine to offer exotic specialities from all over Asia. Even the beer garden serves spring rolls and satay.
🛇 R22 ✉ Maria-Einsiedl-Strasse 2 ☎ 7 23 20 31 🕙 Breakfast buffet Sun from 11am. Restaurant daily lunch, dinner 🚇 U-Bahn Thalkirchen

**MÖVENPICK**
Munich's biggest breakfast is a 30-m (98-ft) long buffet table laden with sumptuous dishes, in a palatial ballroom. Reservations essential.
🛇 N23 ✉ Lenbachplatz 8 ☎ 5 45 94 90 🕙 Mon–Sat 8am–midnight, Sun 9am–midnight 🚇 U- or S-Bahn Karlsplatz

**NEWS BAR**
Catch up on the news over breakfast with a selection of international newspapers and magazines in this smart and popular student meeting place.
🛇 M24 ✉ Amalienstrasse 55 ☎ 28 17 87 🚇 U-Bahn Universität

**SECOND BREAKFAST**

With such a thriving café scene, breakfast in Munich is very much a way of life. There are even a couple of home-delivery breakfast services in town. And, as many people in Munich start their working day very early, they often indulge in a mid-morning snack to bridge the gap between breakfast and lunch, called *Brotzeit* ('bread time'). This may be a sandwich or the traditional local speciality of boiled *Weisswürste* (white sausages) and *Brezen* (knotted rolls sprinkled with coarse grains of salt). There are plenty of opportunities to indulge in *Brotzeit*, whether working in the office, eating on-the-move from a street stall or relaxing in a shady beer garden.

69

# Where to Eat

# Tea, Coffee & Ice-Cream Cafés

## *LEBKÜCHEN* TRADITION

The 600-year-old tradition of baking *Lebküchen* is thought to derive from recipes concocted by monks living in a medieval monastery. The biscuits (cookies), flavoured primarily with almonds, honey and spices, trace their origin back to the honey cakes appreciated by ancient Greeks, Romans and Egyptians, who regarded honey as a gift of the gods. The pre-Christmas season is the busiest time for *Lebküchen* producer, Schmidt, when up to 3 million biscuits are made every day.

### ADAMELLO
Hidden in a quiet backstreet in Haidhausen, this Italian-run café sells the best ice-cream in town. The speciality—*Coppa Adamello*—containing a mountain liquer, is delicious.
025 ✉ Preysingerstrasse 29 ☎ 48 32 83 🕒 Daily 11–6 (midnight in summer) 🚋 Tram 18

### ARZMILLER
A popular post-shopping haunt in a peaceful courtyard near Odeonsplatz.
N24 ✉ Salvatorstrasse 2, Theatinerhof ☎ 29 42 73 🕒 Shop hours 🚇 U-Bahn Odeonsplatz

### CAFÉ LUITPOLD PALMENGARTEN
Chic and pricey, this is next to the ornamental fountain in a most exclusive shopping arcade.
N24 ✉ Brienner Strasse 11 ☎ 2 42 87 50 🕒 Mon–Fri 9–8, Sat 8–7 🚇 U-Bahn Odeonsplatz

### CAFÉ PUCK
A spacious, trendy student haunt in Schwabing. Excellent for breakfast.
M24 ✉ Türkenstrasse 33 ☎ 2 80 22 80 🕒 Daily 9am–1am 🚇 U-Bahn Universität

### DUKATZ IM LITERATURHAUS
This airy, modern café attracts an arty set for weekly poetry readings. The sidewalk terrace is especially popular in summer.
N24 ✉ Salvatorplatz 1 ☎ 29 19 60-0 🕒 Mon–Sat 10am–1am, Sun 10–6 🚇 U-Bahn Odeonsplatz

### KEMPINSKI HOTEL VIER JAHRESZEITEN
One of Munich's top hotels serves a traditional English afternoon tea.
N24 ✉ Maximilianstrasse 17 ☎ 21 25-0 🕒 Daily 2.30–5.30 🚇 U-Bahn Odeonsplatz 🚋 Tram 19

### MÖVENPICK
One of the city's classic coffee-houses. The ice-cream is hard to beat for quality and quantity, with scoops the size of tennis balls.
N23 ✉ Lenbachplatz 8 ☎ 54 59 49-0 🕒 Mon–Sat 8am–midnight, Sun 9–midnight 🚇 U- or S-Bahn Karlsplatz

### SARCLETTIS EIS-ECKE
The largest ice-cream menu in town, with over 100 flavours.
M21 ✉ Nymphenburger Strasse 155 ☎ 15 53 14 🚇 U-Bahn Rotkreuzplatz

### SCHLOSS CAFÉ DACHAU
Heavenly gateaux in a magnificent palace setting.
Off map to northwest ✉ Schlossrate Dachau ☎ (08131) 4543 660 🕒 Daily 9am–10pm 🚆 S-Bahn Dachau

### SCHLOSSCAFÉ IM PALMENHAUS
An elegant café in the Nymphenburg Palace's giant palm house.
L19 ✉ Schloss Nymphenburg ☎ 17 53 09 🕒 Daily 10–5.30 (till 6 in summer) 🚋 Tram 17

# Where to Eat

# Snacks

### BERNI'S NEDELBRETT (€)
A cheap pasta joint. On Saturdays and Sundays from 8pm, during Pasta Happy Hour, the prices drop 50 per cent.
🏠 N24 ✉ Petersplatz 8
☎ 26 44 69 🕐 Daily 11–11
🚇 U- or S-Bahn Marienplatz
🚋 Tram 27

### CAFÉ FRISCHHUT (€)
Early birds meet night owls for strong coffee and delicious deep-fried *Schmalznudeln* doughnuts at 5 in the morning.
🏠 N23 ✉ Prälat-Zistl-Strasse 8
☎ 26 82 37 🕐 Mon–Sat 5am–5pm 🚇 U- or S-Bahn Marienplatz

### MOLLY MALONE (€)
The best fish'n chips in town.
🏠 O25 ✉ Kellerstrasse 21, Haidhausen ☎ 6 88 75 10
🕐 Mon–Fri 5pm–1am, Sat–Sun noon–1am 🚇 S-Bahn Rosenheimerplatz

### MÜNCHNER SCHMANKERL (€)
Hearty Bavarian specialities, including *Weisswurst* and *Leberkäse*, served in big portions, with steaming mugs of *Glühwein* in winter.
🏠 N24 ✉ Viktualienmarkt
🕐 Shop hours 🚇 U- or S-Bahn Marienplatz

### MÜNCHNER SUPPENKÜCHE (€)
Try the *Pfannekuchensuppe* (pancake soup) or *Leberknödelsuppe* (liver dumpling soup) at this soup kitchen.
🏠 N24 ✉ Viktualienmarkt
🕐 Shop hours 🚇 U- or S-Bahn Marienplatz

### NORDSEE (€)
This fishmonger offers a range of hot and cold dishes. Standing room only.
🏠 N24 ✉ Viktualienmarkt
☎ 22 11 86 🕐 Mon–Fri 8–7, Sat 8–4 🚇 U- or S-Bahn Marienplatz

### SUM (€)
A popular shoppers' stop for sushi, dim sum and champagne cocktails, on the top floor of Ludwig Beck department store.
🏠 N24 ✉ Marienplatz 11
☎ 23 69 14 47 🕐 Shop hours
🚇 U- or S-Bahn Marienplatz

### TIRAMISU (€)
This tiny Italian bar serves excellent *antipasti* and has a daily changing pasta menu.
🏠 L23 ✉ Hohenzollernstrasse 124 ☎ 308 60 08 🕐 Mon–Fri 11.30–10, Sat 11.30–5
🚇 U-Bahn Hohenzollernplatz

### VINCENZ MURR (€)
Help yourself at the extensive salad bar, then have a picnic by the fountain opposite.
🏠 N23 ✉ Rosenstrasse 7
☎ 2 60 47 65 🕐 Shop hours
🚇 U- or S-Bahn Marienplatz

### VINI E PANINI (€)
Not only bread and wine but also delicious snacks from different regions of Italy.
🏠 L24 ✉ Nordendstrasse 45
☎ 2 72 17 43 🕐 Mon–Fri 10–6.30, Sat 8–2 🚋 Tram 27

### WOKMAN (€)
Inexpensive and tasty Chinese fast food.
🏠 L24 ✉ Leopoldstrasse 68
☎ 39 03 43 🕐 Daily 11am–midnight 🚇 U-Bahn Münchener Freiheit

## ESSENTIAL SNACKS

The city's countless snackbars (usually called *Kneipe*, *Lokal* or *Schnellimbiss*) and butcher's shops (*Metzgereien*) provide an easy inexpensive way to try traditional Bavarian delicacies, such as *Leberkäs* (a meatloaf of beef, pork and spices), *Kartoffelpuffer* (potato fritters), *Steckerlfisch* (whitefish or mackerel, grilled on a spit), *Radi* (thin slices of salted horseradish) and, of course, sausages. Look out also for *Obatzada*, a soft cheese, mixed with butter, onion, salt, pepper, paprika and caraway, and delicious served with *Brezen*.

## Where to Shop

# Antiques, Design & Books

### BARGAIN-HUNTING

Munich has over 8,000 shops and 15 big department stores and there are plenty of bargains to be had if you know where to look. Start with the department stores that sell cut-price goods in their basements, and always keep your eyes open for *Sonderangebot* (special offer) signs. The best bargains can be found at the end of season sales in January and July, and the discounts can often be astonishing.

### OPENING TIMES

Most shops are open weekdays from 9 until 6.30, with late-night shopping (*Stadtabend*) on Thursdays until 8.30. Don't leave it until Saturday to buy your presents as most shops close at 1 or 2pm, except the first Saturday in every month, when they remain open until 4. However, legislation now permits shops to stay open until 8 on weekdays and until 4 on Saturdays, so opening and closing times are changing around town.

**ANTIKE UHREN EDER**
The silence of this beautiful shop is broken only by the ticking of valuable German timepieces dating from the 19th and early 20th centuries. A must for collectors.
N23 ✉ Prannerstrasse 4 ☎ 22 03 05 Ⓤ U- or S-Bahn Karlsplatz

**LA BELLE EPOQUE**
A mecca for belle epoque collectors, with lamps, clocks, vases, mirrors and other objets d'art from around 1850–1930.
M23 ✉ Augustenstrasse 41 ☎ 52 73 77 Ⓞ Mon–Fri 11–6.30, Sat 10–2 Ⓤ U-Bahn Königsplatz

**DECO SUSANNE KLEIN**
A tiny boutique near Gärtnerplatz, specializing in modern furniture, plush fabrics and state-of-the-art interior design.
O23 ✉ Klenzestrasse 41 ☎ 2 72 24 27 🚋 52, 56

**GLATTEIS**
From John Grisham to Agatha Christie, this small bookshop specializes in 'whodunits' and thrillers.
O24 ✉ Corneliusstrasse 31 ☎ 2 01 48 44 🚋 52, 56

**HUGENDUBEL**
Bookworms love this giant book 'supermarket', spread over four floors. There are sofas where you can sit and read to your heart's content without buying! There are several branches throughout the city.
N24 ✉ Marienplatz 5 ☎ (01801) 48 44 84 Ⓤ U- or S-Bahn Marienplatz

**KOKON**
A magical blend of artefacts, fabrics and furnishings from around the world, with an impressive collection of garden furniture and exotic flowers.
N23 ✉ Lenbachplatz 3 ☎ 5 52 51 40 🚋 Tram 27

**DAS LANDHAUSECK**
A cornucopia of traditional Bavarian furniture and antiques.
N23 ✉ St.-Jacobs-Platz 12 ☎ 260 95 72 Ⓤ U-Bahn Sendlinger Tor

**LANDPARTIE**
A cosy country atmosphere welcomes you into this homely shop, crammed with antique furniture and household accessories.
L24 ✉ Kurfürstenstrasse 12 ☎ 34 85 98 🚋 Tram 27

**ROSENTHAL STUDIO HAUS**
Smart contemporary Rosenthal porcelain and glass, together with Alessi, Orrefors and other choice designer ware.
N24 ✉ Dienerstrasse 17 ☎ 22 26 17 Ⓤ U- or S-Bahn Marienplatz

**WORDSWORTH**
In a picturesque backyard, there is a large range of English books, a Pooh Corner for children and a National Trust shop.
M24 ✉ Schellingstrasse 21a ☎ 2 80 91 41 🚋 53

# Gifts & Bavarian Souvenirs

### ETCETERA
Full of novel Bavarian souvenirs and things you would love to buy but don't really need.
✚ N24 ✉ Wurzerstrasse 12 ☎ 22 60 68 Ⓤ U- or S-Bahn Marienplatz

### GESCHENKE KAISER
Pewter Christmas decorations, serving dishes, candlesticks and beer jugs are the specialities here.
✚ N24 ✉ Rindermarkt 1 ☎ 26 45 09 Ⓤ U- or S-Bahn Marienplatz

### HOLZ UND KLANG
The traditional musical boxes here make a perfect gift to take home.
✚ M16 ✉ Ernsbergerstrasse 5A ☎ 8 34 04 85 Ⓤ S-Bahn Pasing

### I-DÜPFERL
Three floors of tempting ideas for holiday gifts, including fun household gadgets and interesting knick-knacks.
✚ N24 ✉ Im Tal 31 ☎ 2 91 95 70 Ⓤ S-Bahn Isartor

### KUNSTGEWERBE-VEREIN
Shop here for high-quality, carved, painted and handcrafted Bavarian products. Choose from puppets and pottery to jewellery and bright carnival masks—truly exclusive gifts.
✚ N23 ✉ Pacellistrasse 6–8 ☎ 2 90 14 70 Ⓤ U- or S-Bahn Karlsplatz

### LEDERHOSEN WAGNER
This shop has been making Bavaria's distinctive leather shorts from soft deer-skin since 1825. Surprise your friends with a 'shaving brush' hat, made out of chamois hair, to match the shorts.
✚ N24 ✉ Im Tal 2 ☎ 22 56 97 Ⓤ U- or S-Bahn Marienplatz

### LODEN FREY
Choose your *Trachten* (Bavarian folk costume) from the almost endless selection here at the world's largest specialist store for national costume. Children will love the exhilerating toboggan run from the street level to the basement.
✚ N23 ✉ Maffeistrasse 7–9 ☎ 21 03 90 Ⓤ U- or S-Bahn Marienplatz

### MÜNCHNER GESCHENKE-STUBEN
Crammed with every imaginable Bavarian souvenir.
✚ N24 ✉ Petersplatz 8 ☎ 26 74 56 Ⓤ U- or S-Bahn Marienplatz

### STOCKHAMMER
Idea-hungry shoppers are sure to find original gifts here.
✚ L24 ✉ Hohenzollernstrasse 33 ☎ 34 15 77 Ⓤ U- or S-Bahn Münchener Freiheit

### WALLACH
This famous rococo-fronted shop is full of Bavarian atmosphere and attractive gifts, including fantastic hand-printed fabrics and colourful *Dirndls* (▶ panel).
✚ N24 ✉ Residenzstrasse 3 ☎ 2 20 87 10 Ⓤ U- or S-Bahn Marienplatz

---

***TRACHTEN* AND MORE**

The nice thing about *Trachten* (Bavarian folk costume) is that Münchners really do wear it, especially on Sundays, holidays or festive occasions. Most popular are the *Lederhosen* and the smart green-collared grey jackets for men or the gaily-coloured *Dirndl* dresses with fitted bodices and full gathered skirts.

## Where to Shop

# Department Stores, Food Stores & Markets

### CELEBRATING IN STYLE

When Paul and Elsa Käfer opened a modest food and wine shop in Munich in 1930, they had no idea that their name would become synonymous with the stylish parties that their son would arrange, in the more prosperous 1960s, for film stars and other prominent members of post-war high society. The store survives as a food lover's paradise and the catering side of the business now supplies museums and restaurants including the rooftop restaurant of the renovated German parliament building (Reichstag) in Berlin.

**BAGEL SHOP**
Choose from sesame, garlic, onion, raisin, blueberry, pumpernickel and plain, with toppings ranging from smoked salmon and sour cream to pastrami and tomato. Also muffins, brownies and cookies.
M23 ✉ Barerstrasse 72 ☎ 2 71 21 86 🚋 Tram 27

**BOETTNER**
One of Munich's oldest hostelries is well known for its schnapps, caviar and other delicacies.
N24 ✉ Pfisterstrasse 9 ☎ 22 12 10 Ⓤ U- or S-Bahn Marienplatz

**DALLMAYR**
The city's top delicatessen used to supply the Bavarian royal family. The first floor serves a lovely champagne breakfast.
N24 ✉ Dienerstrasse 14-15 ☎ 2 13 50 Ⓤ U- or S-Bahn Marienplatz

**EILLES**
One of several Eilles stores, selling fine tea, coffee and wines.
N24 ✉ Residenzstrasse 13 ☎ 22 61 84 Ⓤ U- or S-Bahn Marienplatz

**ELISABETHMARKT**
Schwabing's *Viktualienmarkt*, with surprisingly few tourists.
L23 ✉ Elisabethplatz 🚋 Tram 27

**ELLY SEIDL**
A tiny chocolate shop, famous for its pralines and its *Münchner Kuppeln* chocolates, which look like the onion-domes of the Frauenkirche.
N24 ✉ Am Kosttor 2 ☎ 22 15 22 Ⓤ U- or S-Bahn Marienplatz

**HERTIE**
This branch of the Hertie department store chain stretches from the main train station to Karlsplatz and offers everyday items at reasonable prices.
N23 ✉ Bahnhofplatz ☎ 5 51 20 Ⓤ U- or S-Bahn Hauptbahnhof

**KÄFER**
An epicurean labyrinth selling food and drink from around the world in the smart Bogenhausen district.
N25
✉ Prinzregentenstrasse 73 ☎ 4 16 80 Ⓤ U-Bahn Prinzregentenplatz

**KARSTADT**
This giant department store has three main outlets: Haus Oberpollinger am Dom sells electical appliances, books and furnishings; Karstadt am Karlstor offers cosmetics and clothing; Karstadt Sporthaus Oberpollinger stocks sports items.
N23 ✉ Neuhauser Strasse 18 ☎ 29 02 30 Ⓤ U- or S-Bahn Karlsplatz

**KAUFHOF**
One of several Kaufhof department stores here; centrally located.
N24 ✉ Kaufingerstrasse 1–5 ☎ 23 18 51 Ⓤ U- or S-Bahn Marienplatz

**LA MAISON DU VIN**
There is an exceptional range of fine French wines here.

74

# Where to Shop

🏠 N23 ✉ Prälat-Zistlstrasse 4 ☎ 26 32 82 🚌 52, 56

## LE CHALET DU FROMAGE
One of Munich's best cheesemongers.
🏠 L24 ✉ Stand 11, Elisabethplatz ☎ 2 71 22 43 🕐 Closed Mon 🚊 Tram 27

## LUDWIG BECK
Beck is without doubt Munich's most stylish department store, a Munich institution with a changing decor created by well-known artists. At Christmas artisans work on the top floor and the store becomes a winter wonderland of handicrafts. Round off your visit with a snack at the oriental Sum Bar.
🏠 N24 ✉ Marienplatz 11 ☎ 23 69 10 🚇 U- or S-Bahn Marienplatz

## MARKT AM WIENER PLATZ
Tiny green wooden produce stands huddle around the maypole in Haidhausen—an attractive alternative to the supermarket.
🏠 N25 ✉ Wiener Platz 🚇 U-Bahn Max-Weber-Platz

## OLYMPIA EINKAUFSZENTRUM (OEZ)
For everything under one roof, visit this huge shopping complex with over 100 shops near the Olympiapark.
🏠 H21 ✉ Hanauerstrasse 68 ☎ 1 41 60 61 🚌 36

## RISCHART
One of many Rischart shops offers the largest choice of bread, rolls and cakes in town.
🏠 N24 ✉ Marienplatz 18 ☎ 2 31 70 00 🚇 U- or S-Bahn Marienplatz

## SCHMIDT
Shop here for some of the best *Lebküchen* (delicious spice cookies), which are presented in collectable tins, along with *Stollen* (fruitcakes).
🏠 N24 ✉ Westenriederstrasse 6 ☎ 29 50 68 🚇 S-Bahn Isartor

## SPANISCHES FRUCHTHAUS
A mouth-watering display of dried fruits entices you into this small shop with an unusual selection of crystallized, fresh and chocolate-coated fruits.
🏠 N23 ✉ Rindermarkt 10 ☎ 26 45 70 🚇 U- or S-Bahn Marienplatz

## SPORT-SCHECK
The department store for sports fanatics. Six floors are dedicated to every sport imaginable. You can even arrange sporting activities or a day-long ski trip on the sixth floor.
🏠 N23 ✉ Sendlingerstrasse 6 ☎ 21 66-0 🚇 U-Bahn Sendlinger Tor

## VIKTUALIENMARKT
The largest and most famous Bavarian open-air food market is near the bustling city centre. Look out for the Kräuterstand Freisinger stand for Alpine herbs and the Honighäusl stand for honey products.
🏠 N24 🕐 Mon–Fri 7.30–6, Sat 7.30–1 🚇 U- or S-Bahn Marienplatz

## FLEA MARKETS

Flea markets have long been a tradition in Munich, offering fun shopping either in the small impromptu markets or in the large, well-organized, commercial ones in Arnulfstrasse or in the grounds of the Pfanni factory on the east side of Munich. One of Munich's largest and most popular markets takes place at the Theresienwiese on the first day of the *Frühlingsfest* (Spring Festival) in April.

## Where to Shop

# Specialist Shops

## TOYS

Germany has been one of the world's leading toy manufacturers since the Middle Ages, and is particularly famous for its china dolls, tin plate toys and Steiff teddy bears. Many important manufacturing areas are around Munich–Nuremberg, Oberammergau and Berchtesgaden. Today, old Steiff bears are considered great collector's pieces; the record is for Teddy Girl, which was sold for £110,000 at auction in December 1994.

### BEAUTYSPY
A pot pourri of bathtime products and fun cosmetics. Treat yourself to a 'Spa in a Bottle' or a 'Pamper Pack'.
✚ N23 ✉ Maffeistrasse 6 ☎ 24 24 38 64 🚊 Tram 19

### BREE
Smart suitcases, belts, handbags and more.
✚ N24 ✉ Theatinerhof, Salvatorstrasse 2 ☎ 29 87 45 Ⓤ U-Bahn Odeonplatz

### CENTURY BOX
A veritable emporium of collectibles from the 1950s to the 1980s.
✚ O25 ✉ Steinstrasse 73 ☎ 0172-8951669 Ⓤ S-Bahn Rosenheimer Platz

### DEHNER
Full of great gift ideas for garden lovers. What about a packet of Alpine flower seeds or even a grow-your-own 'Bavarian meadow'?
✚ N24 ✉ Frauenstrasse 8 ☎ 24 23 99 80 Ⓤ S-Bahn Isartor

### DIE PUPPENSTUBE
Dolls and puppets to take you back to your childhood.
✚ M23 ✉ Luisenstrasse 68 ☎ 272 32 67 🚊 53

### FOURTH DIMENSION
One of Germany's leading costume jewellery shops. Smart but affordable.
✚ N23 ✉ Frauenplatz 14 ☎ 22 80 10 90 Ⓤ S-Bahn Marienplatz

### GOOD STUFF
Everything for skaters–skateboards, rollerblades, ice-skates, 'tricks' videos and a host of cool clothing and accessories.
✚ L24 ✉ Occamstrasse 15 ☎ 39 11 22 Ⓤ U-Bahn Münchener Freiheit

### HEMMERLE
The treasures in this traditional Munich jeweller are expensive but very solid.
✚ N24 ✉ Maximilianstrasse 14 ☎ 2 42 26 00 🚊 Tram 19

### KAUT-BULLINGER
Three floors of chic stationery ranging from pens, writing paper and art materials to leather personal organizers and designer wrapping paper.
✚ N23 ✉ Rosenstrasse 8 ☎ 23 80 00 Ⓤ U-or S-Bahn Marienplatz

### KREMER PIGMENTE
A tiny shop opposite the Neue Pinakothek selling over 500 different colours for artists of every medium from oils to watercolours, together with paper and brushes.
✚ M23 ✉ Barerstrasse 46 ☎ 28 54 88 🚊 Tram 27

### KUNST UND SPIEL
A magical shop full of sturdy, educational toys together with an extensive arts and craft section.
✚ L24 ✉ Leopoldstrasse 48 ☎ 3 81 62 70 Ⓤ U-Bahn Giselastrasse

### LEUTE—ALLES AUS HOLZ
Everything here is made of wood, with decorative and functional items ranging from games to

# Where to Shop

biscuit cutters.
🅽 N24  ✉ Viktualienmarkt 15
☎ 26 82 48  🚇 U- or S-Bahn Marienplatz

### LUDWIG BECK
The fifth floor of this exclusive department store boasts Germany's largest jazz selection, with over 25,000 CDs to choose from.
🅽 N24  ✉ Marienplatz 11
☎ 23 69 10  🚇 U- or S-Bahn Marienplatz

### MAX HIEBER AM DOM
One of the best bets in Munich for CDs, tapes and sheet music.
🅽 N23  ✉ Liebfrauenstrasse 1
☎ 2 90 08 00  🚇 U- or S-Bahn Marienplatz

### MESSER & SCHEREN
A specialist knife and scissor shop–excellent for left-handers too.
🅽 025  ✉ Rosenheimerstrasse 42  ☎ 4 80 13 92  🚇 S-Bahn Rosenheimer Platz

### MUSEUMSLADEN DEUTSCHES MUSEUM
An amazing, eccentric shop full of books, toys, puzzles and models based on the scientific and technical world, for children and adults.
🅽 024  ✉ Museumsinsel 1
☎ 21 38 38 92  🚇 S-Bahn Isartor  🚋 Tram 18

### OBLETTER
Comprehensive toy shop selling everything from cuddly toys to train sets. Other branches.
🅽 N23  ✉ Karlsplatz 11–12
☎ 55 08 95 10  🚇 U- or S-Bahn Karlsplatz

### PERLENMARKT
This unique shop sells nothing but buttons, beads and jewellery-making equipment.
🅽 L24  ✉ Nordendstrasse 28
☎ 2 71 05 76  🚋 Tram 27

### PORZELLAN-MANUFAKTUR NYMPHENBUR
This famous porcelain manufacturer still turns out traditional rococo designs. Based in Nymphenburg Palace, with this outlet in the heart of the city.
🅽 N24  ✉ Odeonsplatz 1
☎ 28 24 28  🕐 Mon–Fri 10–6.30, Sat 10–4
🚇 U-Bahn Odeonsplatz

### 2-RAD
This shop has everything a bicycle fanatic could possibly want. A second branch round the corner specializes in cycling with children.
🅽 L24  ✉ Georgenstrasse 39
☎ 2 71 63 83  🚋 Tram 27

### SCHREIBMAYR
Beautiful desk equipment, handmade paper and pens for lovers of the art of letter writing, together with ink in every imaginable shade, including 'King Ludwig's ink'.
🅽 N24  ✉ Theatinerstrasse 11 (in den Fünf Höfen)  ☎ 2 19 98 40  🚇 U- or S-Bahn Marienplatz

### UNIVERBLÜMT
Say it with flowers! Munich boasts some eye-catching florists and at this one, owned by a fashion designer, each bouquet is a work of art.
🅽 N24  ✉ Liebherrstrasse 8
☎ 2 28 59 96  🚇 S-Bahn Isartor

### HAND-CRAFTED PORCELAIN

The manufacture of exquisite porcelain figurines and dishes was started in 1747 by Prince Elector Maximilian III Joseph at his Nymphenburg Palace (► 26) in suburban Munich. Today about 85 artists and artisans keep alive traditional methods at a cramped factory across from the palace, throwing, forming and painting each piece by hand. Their delicate creations range from bowls and cups to graceful dancers and animals.

## Where to Shop

# Fashion Shops

### HIGH STREET FASHION

In recent years, traditional department stores have concentrated more on fashion and high technology in an attempt to win back the affluent shoppers who have switched their patronage to trendy boutiques and specialist retailers. The stores are offering more upmarket merchandise while weeding out everyday household goods and items that attract low profit margins.

**BEHRINGER**
Fine shoes and accessories for men and women, from Prada to Jimmy Choo, in one of Germany's top shoe shops.
N24 ✉ Salvatorplatz 4 ☎ 29 59 55 U-Bahn Odeonsplatz

**BOGNER**
This classic Munich company sells everything from sports clothes to traditional costumes for both men and women.
N24 ✉ Residenzstrasse 15 ☎ 2 90 70 40 U- or S-Bahn Marienplatz

**EDUARD MEIER**
Munich's oldest shoe shop, established in 1596, with leather sofas and first-class service.
N24 ✉ Residenzstrasse 22 ☎ 22 00 44 U- or S-Bahn Marienplatz

**ESCADA**
Escada was the first national designer label to make it big outside Germany and remains a classic, quintessentially German favourite.
N24 ✉ Maximilianstrasse 27 ☎ 24 23 98 80 Tram 19

**HALLHUBER**
Leading labels at reasonable prices. Hallhuber is popular with young shoppers.
L24 ✉ Leopoldstrasse 25 ☎ 24 22 42 06 U-Bahn Münchener Freiheit

**HIRMER**
A first-class clothing shop with six floors exclusively for men.
N23 ✉ Kaufingerstrasse 28 ☎ 23 68 30 U- or S-Bahn Marienplatz

**KONEN**
A reliable fashion shop full of leading international labels.
N23 ✉ Sendlingerstrasse 3 ☎ 2 44 42 20 U-Bahn Sendlinger Tor

**PATAGONIA**
Stylish but practical sports clothing.
L24 ✉ Leopoldstrasse 47 ☎ 39 92 99 U-Bahn Münchener Freiheit

**RUDOLF MOSHAMMER**
Flamboyant menswear designs of eccentric couturier Rudolf Moshammer draw sheiks and princes to his boutique, with master-pieces in silk, velvet and satin.
N24 ✉ Maximilianstrasse 14 ☎ 22 69 24 Tram 19

**SCHLICHTING**
A vast choice of fashion items for children, teens and mothers-to-be, along with toys and games.
N24 ✉ Weinstrasse 8 ☎ 2 10 38 70 U- or S-Bahn Marienplatz

**STRUMPFHAUS LUDWIG BECK**
Lovely lingerie, as well as stockings and socks in every imaginable shade.
N24 ✉ Dienerstrasse 21, am Rathauseck ☎ 23 69 10 U- or S-Bahn Marienplatz

**THERESA**
Trendy and wildly expensive designer fashions, mainly Italian *prêt-à-porter*.
N24 ✉ Maffeistrasse 3 ☎ 22 48 45 U-Bahn Odeonsplatz

# Cinemas & Nightclubs

## CINEMAS

### ARRI KINO
One of Munich's main arthouse cinemas.
🕀 M24 ✉ Türkenstrasse 91 ☎ 38 89 96 64 🚇 U-Bahn Universität

### CINEMA
Probably the best cinema in town, with four different films daily, mostly undubbed.
🕀 M22 ✉ Nymphenburger Strasse 31 ☎ 55 52 55 🚇 U-Bahn Stiglmaierplatz

### IMAX
Germany's first IMAX cinema shows nature films on a giant screen.
🕀 024 ✉ Forum am Deutsches Museum, Museumsinsel 1 ☎ 21 12 50 🚇 S-Bahn Isartor

### MÜNCHNER FILMMUSEUM
Daily screenings from Germany's largest collection of silent movies. Within the Stadtmuseum (➤ 38) the Filmmuseum stages a competition for European Film Colleges every November.
🕀 N23 ✉ St.-Jakobs-Platz 1 ☎ 23 32 23 48 🚇 U-Bahn Sendlinger Tor, U- or S-Marienplatz

### MUSEUM LICHTSPIELE
This former music-hall frequently shows English-language films.
🕀 024 ✉ Lilienstrasse 2 ☎ 48 24 03 🚇 S-Bahn Rosenheimerplatz 🚋 Tram 18

## NIGHTCLUBS

### ATOMIC CAFÉ
An 'in' club, frequented by a young, ultra-cool crowd, with the musical emphasis on BritPop.
🕀 N24 ✉ Neuturmstrasse 5 ☎ 2 28 30 54 🕐 Tue–Sun 10pm–3am (Fri, Sat till 4) 🚇 U- or S-Bahn Marienplatz 🚋 Tram 19

### KULT FABRIK
A hip nightlife complex, housed in an old factory complex. Huge on the all-night party scene with 25 bars and clubs to suit all musical tastes.
🕀 O26 ✉ Grafingerstrasse 6 ☎ 49 00 29 28 🕐 10.30pm–4am 🚇 U- or S-Bahn Ostbahnhof

### NACHTWERK
Former warehouse with plenty of dance space; popular for live bands.
🕀 N20 ✉ Landsbergerstrasse 185 ☎ 578 38 00 🕐 10.30pm–4am 🚇 S-Bahn Donnersbergerbrücke 🚋 Tram 18, 19

### P1
Extremely chic club in the basement of the Haus der Kunst (➤ 56). Eight different bars frequented by models and celebrities.
🕀 M24 ✉ Prinzregentenstrasse 1 ☎ 29 42 52 🕐 11pm–4am 🚇 U-Bahn Lehel

### PARK CAFÉ
Popular club with music for all tastes in an unlikely rococo setting.
🕀 N23 ✉ Sophienstrasse 7 ☎ 59 83 13 🕐 Tue–Thu 10pm–4am 🚇 U-Bahn Königsplatz

### SKYLINE
New York-style bar and dance club with breathtaking views.
🕀 L24 ✉ Leopoldstrasse 82 ☎ 33 31 31 🕐 6.30pm–4am 🚇 U-Bahn Münchener Freiheit

---

## Where to be Entertained

### CINEMATIC EVENTS

It is hardly surprising that Munich is a city of cinema-goers, with the Bavaria Film Studios, 84 cinemas and a series of film festivals, including a Documentary Film Festival in April, the major *Münchner Filmfest* in Gasteig in June/July, a Fantasy Film Festival in July and International Art Film Week in August. The European Film Colleges Festival rounds off the year in November.

## Where to be Entertained

# Bars, Cafés & Live Music

### ALL-NIGHT PARTYING

Compared with other major European cities, Munich's nightlife is relatively small-scale and provincial–due to early-closing laws that prevent many places from staying open all night. Nevertheless, if you know where to go you can party until the early hours. Many bars close around 1am and most nightclubs at 4am. However, the Backstage Club, nicknamed 'House of the Rising Sun', with its techno and house music sometimes doesn't even *open* until 6am.

### CAFÉ AM BEETHOVENPLATZ
Munich's oldest 'concert-café', combines the atmosphere of an old-style Viennese coffee house with a Bavarian-style beer garden, with live music most evenings.
🗺 022 ✉ Goethestrasse 51 ☎ 54 40 43 48 🕐 9am–1am 🚇 U-Bahn Goetheplatz 🚌 58

### CAFÉ GLOCKENSPIEL
Opposite Marienplatz's famous Glockenspiel, the roof-terrace cocktail bar, plush baroque-style bar and 1970s-style Expresso bar-café here are always crowded.
🗺 N24 ✉ Marienplatz 28 (5th floor) ☎ 26 42 56 🕐 10am–1am 🚇 U- or S-Bahn Marienplatz

### CAFÉ NEUHAUSEN
Mingle with the in-crowd at this stylish café with its long list of long drinks.
🗺 M21 ✉ Blutenbergstrasse 106 ☎ 1 23 62 88 🕐 10am–1am 🚇 U-Bahn Rotkreuzplatz

### HAUS DER 111 BIERE
The name 'House of 111 Beers', speaks for itself.
🗺 L24 ✉ Franzstrasse 3 ☎ 33 12 48 🕐 Mon–Thu 5pm–midnight, Fri–Sat 5pm–3am 🚇 U-Bahn Münchener Freiheit

### HAVANNA CLUB
Ernest Hemingway used to drink in this dark, intimate bar decorated in Spanish colonial style.
🗺 N24 ✉ Herrnstrasse 30 ☎ 29 18 84 🕐 Mon–Wed 6–1, Thu–Sat 6–2, Sun 7–1 🚇 S-Bahn Isartor

### INTERVIEW
A stylish crowd frequents this modern American bar from early morning till late at night.
🗺 024 ✉ Gärtnerplatz 1 ☎ 2 02 16 49 🕐 10–1.30am (Sun till 7am) 🚌 52, 56

### JAZZCLUB UNTERFAHRT
One of Europe's most important jazz clubs featuring modern jazz, bebop and avant-garde names.
🗺 026 ✉ Einsteinstrasse 44 ☎ 4 48 27 94 🕐 Sun–Thu 7.30pm–1am, Fri–Sat 7.30pm–3am 🚇 U-Bahn Max-Weber-Platz 🚋 Tram 19

### JODLER WIRT
This folksy, tiny bar is straight out of the Bavarian countryside—always crowded and jolly, often with local yodellers at night.
🗺 N24 ✉ Altenhofstrasse 4 ☎ 22 12 49 🕐 Mon–Sat 7pm–3am 🚇 U- or S-Bahn Marienplatz

### JULEPS NEW YORK BAR
Spend 'happy hour' here (5–8pm) with a choice of over 150 cocktails.
🗺 025 ✉ Breisacherstrasse 18 ☎ 4 48 00 44 🕐 7pm–1am 🚇 S-Bahn Ostbahnhof

### MORIZZ
This plush bar draws a cool, and often gay clientele, for cocktails and sophisticated snacks.
🗺 023 ✉ Klenzestrasse 43 ☎ 2 01 67 76 🕐 7pm–2am (Fri–Sat till 3am) 🚇 U-Bahn Fraunhoferstrasse 🚌 52, 56

## Where to be Entertained

### KAFFEE GIESING
Excellent live music, particularly jazz, blues and rock, and classical music for breakfast.
Q23 ✉ Bergstrasse 5 ☎ 6 92 05 79 🕐 Mon–Fri 4pm–1am, Sat 11am–1am, Sun 11am–3pm Ⓤ U-Bahn Silberhornstrasse

### KSAR-CLUB
Hugely popular bar in the trendy Gärtnerplatz district, complete with stylish clientele, expensive cocktails and music to suit all tastes.
023 ✉ Müllerstrasse 31 ☎ 26 40 38 🕐 8pm–3am Ⓤ U-Bahn Sendlinger Tor 🚋 Tram 18, 20

### MASTER'S HOME
An extraordinary underground bar in the colonial style of a typical African farmhouse. You can sit in the bathroom, the bedroom, the living room or at the bar, which is cooled by a giant aeroplane propeller, and eat, dance or simply lap up the atmosphere over a delicious cocktail.
N24 ✉ Frauenstrasse 11 ☎ 22 99 09 🕐 6pm–3am, Sun 11am–3pm Ⓢ S-Bahn Isartor

### MISTER B'S
A small atmospheric jazz bar with daily live concerts at 10pm.
022 ✉ Herzog-Heinrich-Strasse 38 ☎ 53 49 01 🕐 Tue–Sun 8pm–3am Ⓤ U-Bahn Goetheplatz

### NACHT CAFÉ
This 1950s-style bar is one of Munich's most popular places for live music ranging from jazz and blues to flamenco.
N23 ✉ Maximiliansplatz 5 ☎ 59 59 00 🕐 8pm–6am Ⓤ U- or S-Bahn Karlsplatz

### ODODO
A simple, stylish bar, appealing to a diverse clientele, for its unusual mix of fondues and exotic cocktails.
O24 ✉ Buttermelcherstrasse 6 ☎ (08) 260 77 41 🕐 Mon–Thu 11am–1am, Fri 11am–3am, Sat 6pm–3am, Sun 6pm–1am 🚋 52, 56

### OKLAHOMA
Authentic saloon bar with live country-and-western music.
R22 ✉ Schäftlarnstrasse 156 ☎ 7 23 43 27 🕐 Wed–Sat 7–1am Ⓤ U-Bahn Thalkirchen

### PODIUM
A small, popular venue that does rock'n roll and blues.
L24 ✉ Wagnerstrasse 1 ☎ 39 94 82 🕐 Mon–Fri 8pm–1am, Sat–Sun 8pm–3am Ⓤ U-Bahn Münchener Freiheit

### SCHUMANN'S
It's hard to get a table here at Germany's number-one bar, but once inside you can enjoy watching Munich's *Schickeria* (the chic set) at play.
N24 ✉ Odeonsplatz 6 ☎ 22 90 60 🕐 Mon–Fri 5pm–3am, Sun 6pm–3am 🚋 Tram 19

### WEINHAUS
A cozy venue for wine connoisseurs.
M24 ✉ Amalienstrasse 53 ☎ 28 58 90 🕐 Mon–Fri 11.30am–3pm, 6.30–midnight Ⓤ U-Bahn Universität

### BEER GARDENS
The Bavarian capital city's renowned beer gardens (▶ 52–53) thrive from the first warm days of spring to the annual drinking climax of the Oktoberfest (▶ 54), when they are augmented by huge party tents erected on a city centre meadow (*Theresienwiese*). Before electrical refrigeration was invented, brewers planted chestnut trees above their storage cellars to help keep supplies cool, then put out tables and benches in the shade to welcome drinkers. To this day, the spring-flowering of the chestnut trees heralds the start of the beer garden season.

Where to be Entertained

# Theatre, Classical Music, Opera & Ballet

## MUSICAL MECCA

Munich and music go hand-in-hand. The city's connection with Mozart, Wagner and Richard Strauss, not to mention its three symphony orchestras, has made it famous throughout the world. Today, it plays host to major events in the musical calendar including the glamorous Opera Festival and the Summer Concert Season at Nymphenburg Palace. Try also to attend one of the summer open-air concerts at the Residenz, held in an atmospheric courtyard setting.

### CUVILLIÉS THEATER
Both opera and drama are popular at this magnificent theatre, venue for the première of Mozart's *Idomeneo*, and considered the finest rococo theatre in the world.
✚ N24  ✉ Residenzstrasse 1
☎ 29 68 36  Ⓤ U-Bahn Odeonsplatz

### DAS SCHLOSS
Great theatre classics are performed all year round in a giant tent on the outskirts of the Olympiapark.
✚ K22  ✉ Schwere-Reiter-Strasse 15  ☎ 3 00 30 13
🚋 Tram 27

### DEUTSCHES THEATER
The number-one venue for musicals, revues and ballet.
✚ N23  ✉ Schwanthalerstrasse 13  ☎ 55 23 44 44  Ⓤ U- or S-Bahn Karlsplatz

### GASTEIG
Home of the Munich Philharmonic Orchestra and the city's main cultural centre (➤ 83, panel).
✚ O25  ✉ Rosenheimerstrasse 5  ☎ 48 09 80  Ⓤ S-Bahn Rosenheimer Platz

### HERKULESSAAL
Munich's most impressive concert hall, in the Residenz.
✚ N24  ✉ Residenzstrasse 1
☎ 29 16 06 83  Ⓤ U-Bahn Odeonsplatz

### HOCHSCHULE FÜR MUSIK
Young up-and-coming musicians from the Music Academy give regular free evening concerts and lunchtime recitals. Call for details.
✚ M23  ✉ Arcisstrasse 12
☎ 28 92 74 42  Ⓤ U-Bahn Königsplatz

### KOMÖDIE IM BAYERISCHEN HOF
Sophisticated light comedy is the speciality here.
✚ N23  ✉ Promenadeplatz 6
☎ 29 28 10  Ⓤ U- or S-Bahn Karlsplatz

### LACH UND SCHIESS-GESELLSCHAFT
Germany's most satirical revues are performed here.
✚ L25  ✉ Haimhauser-Ursulastrasse Ecke  ☎ 39 19 97
Ⓤ U-Bahn Münchener Freiheit

### MÜNCHNER KAMMERSPIELE
The 'Munich Playhouse' is considered one of Germany's best theatres. Tickets are like gold dust.
✚ N24  ✉ Falkenbergstrasse 2
☎ 23 33 70 00  Ⓤ U- or S-Bahn Marienplatz

### MÜNCHNER MARIONETTEN-THEATER
A delightful puppet theatre with shows especially for children in the afternoons and marionette opera performances for adults in the evenings.
✚ O23  ✉ Blumenstrasse 32
☎ 26 57 12  Ⓤ U-Bahn Sendlinger Tor

### MÜNCHNER SOMMERTHEATER
Each July the Munich Summer Theatre presents a series of popular open-air

## Where to be Entertained

performances in the English Garden's amphitheatre.
🟥 K26 ✉ Rümelinstraße 8 ☎ 98 93 88 🚇 U-Bahn Alte Heide 🚌 Bus 87

### MÜNCHNER THEATER FÜR KINDER
The German language proves no barrier for children in this magical theatre where fairy tales come alive. Favourites include Pinocchio and Hänsel and Gretel.
🟥 M22 ✉ Dachauerstrasse 46 ☎ 59 54 54 🚇 U-Bahn Stiglmaierplatz

### NATIONALTHEATER (BAVARIAN STATE OPERA)
The Nationaltheater is one of Europe's most respected opera-houses. The excellent opera festival in July is the high point of Munich's cultural year.
🟥 N24 ✉ Max-Joseph-Platz 2 ☎ 2185-1920 🚇 U- or S-Bahn Marienplatz

### PRINZREGENTEN-THEATER
This theatre was originally built to emulate the famous Wagner Festspielhaus in Bayreuth in 1900. Today it stages plays, concerts, opera and musicals.
🟥 N25 ✉ Prinzregentenplatz 12 ☎ 21 85 28 99 🚇 U-Bahn Prinzregentenplatz

### RESIDENZTHEATER
A modern theatre with a broad repertoire of classical and contemporary plays.
🟥 N24 ✉ Max-Joseph-Platz 1 ☎ 21 85 01 🚇 U-Bahn Odeonsplatz

### SCHLOSS BLUTENBURG
Popular chamber music venue in an atmospheric 15th-century moated castle (➤ 59).
🟥 L16 ✉ Obermenzing ☎ 8 34 44 45 🚇 S-Bahn Obermenzing

### STAATSTHEATER AM GÄRTNERPLATZ
This flourishing theatre claims to be the only municipal light opera-house in the world, with a wide repertoire of operetta, light opera, musicals and ballet.
🟥 O24 ✉ Gärtnerplatz 3 ☎ 2 01 67 67 🚇 U-Bahn Fraunhoferstrasse

### THEATER BEI HEPPEL & ETTLICH
A relaxed atmosphere and a glass of beer welcomes you to this student bar-cum-theatre.
🟥 L24 ✉ Kaiserstrasse 67 ☎ 34 93 59 🚊 Tram 12, 27

### THEATER DER JUGEND
Shows here appeal to both small children (morning and afternoon performances) and teenagers (evening).
🟥 L24 ✉ Schanburg Franz-Joseph-Strasse 47 ☎ 23 33 71 71 🚇 U-Bahn Giselastrasse or Josephsplatz

### THEATER IM MARSTALL
Avant-garde theatre and experimental performances by the State Opera and the Residenztheater company.
🟥 N24 ✉ Marstallplatz ☎ 21 85 19 20 🚇 U-Bahn Odeonsplatz

### GASTEIG
This modern cultural, educational and conference complex lies at the heart of Munich's music scene, focused on its splendid concert hall with its much-praised acoustics. There are concerts in the Carl-Orff-Saal, and during weekday lunchtimes students of the resident Richard Strauss Conservatory give free recitals in the Kleine Konzertsaal. Gasteig also houses Germany's largest city library and is the venue for the annual Film Festival, along with a full programme of dance, experimental theatre, films and jazz.

Where to be Entertained

# Sport & Activities

**OUTDOOR MUNICH**

The Englischer Garten (English Garden, ➤ 49) is a popular place for Munich's city dwellers to walk, cycle or sunbathe. This extensive green space stretches from the middle of the city along the banks of the River Isar. The Olympiapark (➤ 27), the stadium site of the 1972 Olympic Games, has been converted into a much-loved and much-used park with facilities including swimming, tennis and ice-skating.

## PARTICIPANT SPORTS

### BLADE NIGHTS
Join tens of thousands of local roller-blader fanatics touring the city on 'Blade Nights', every Monday night from May to September. Check on www.muenchner-blade-night.de for times and route details.
➕ N22 ✉ Start in Theresienhöhe (behind the statue of Bavaria) 🚇 U-Bahn Theresienwiese

### DER REISEBÜRO
Contact this travel agent to reserve one of Bavaria's most enjoyable boating experiences. On a *Gaudiflossenfahrt*, a pleasure raft trip on the River Isar from Wolfratshausen to Thalkirchen, you will drift downstream in a convoy to the music of a brass band and a steady flow of beer from the barrels on board. The highlight of the day is the waterslide.
➕ N22 ✉ Bahnhofplatz 2 ☎ 55140-200 🚇 U- or S-Bahn Hauptbahnhof

### BLUE UP
Don't let the name put you off this trip of a lifetime in a hot-air balloon, guaranteeing exceptional views of the Alps.
➕ Off map to south ✉ Buchenerstrasse 25, Bad Tölz ☎ (08041) 7933722 🚉 Bad Tölz (➤ 21)

### BUNGEE JUMPING JOCHEN SCHWEIZER
Get a new perspective on Munich, hanging upside-down from a bridge.
➕ 026 ✉ Grafingerstrasse 6 ☎ 6 06 08 90 🚇 S-Bahn Ostbahnhof

### DANTEBAD
Swim while it snows at this outdoor pool—open all year.
➕ K21 ✉ Postillonstrasse 17 ☎ (01801) 796223 🚌 83, 177

### DEUTSCHER ALPENVEREIN
This Alpine walkers' club organizes walking excursions in the mountains. Why not tackle the nearby Zugspitze, Germany's highest mountain?
➕ N24 ✉ Von-Kahr-Strasse 2–4 ☎ 14 00 30 🚋 Tram 17, 19

### ELIXIA-PRINZ
Pump iron at one of Munich's trendiest fitness centres.
➕ N26 ✉ Prinzregentenplatz 9 ☎ 41 20 02 00 🚇 U-Bahn Prinzregentenplatz

### FELDAFING GOLF CLUB
One of the finest golf courses in Germany, overlooking Starnberger See.
➕ Off map to southwest ✉ Tutzingerstrasse 15, Feldafing ☎ (08157) 93340 🚇 S-Bahn Feldafing

### ISAR-BOWLING
One of Munich's biggest ten-pin bowling alleys, with special 'Moonlight-Disco-Bowling' at weekends.
➕ Q24 ✉ Martin-Luther-Strasse 22 ☎ 6 92 45 12 🚇 U-Bahn Silberhornstrasse

### MARIENHOF ICE RINK
Skating under the stars

## Where to be Entertained

on an outdoor ice-rink, on a crisp winter's evening, is a truly magical experience. Skate rental is available, and the rink is surrounded by stands selling such snacks as toasted chestnuts and steaming *Glühwein*.
🗺 N24 ✉ Marienhof 🕐 Late Nov–end Jan daily 10.30–10 🚇 U- or S-Bahn Marienplatz

### MAX SCHROPP
Learn to windsurf on the Starnberger See, or rent a sailing boat to explore this beautiful lake with its Alpine backdrop.
🗺 Off map to south ✉ Seepromenade Boothaus 4, Starnberg ☎ (08151) 12586 🚇 S-Bahn Starnberg

### MÜLLER'SCHES VOLKSBAD
Germany's loveliest indoor swimming pool, in the Jugendstil style.
🗺 O24 ✉ Rosenheimer Strasse 1 ☎ (01801) 796223 🚇 Tram 18 🚇 S-Bahn Isartor

### OLYMPIA-EISSTADION
Try your hand at curling, a traditional Alpine sport, held on Thursday evenings at the Olympic Ice Stadium.
🗺 J22 ☎ 30 67-0 🚇 U-Bahn Olympiazentrum

### OLYMPIC PARK ICE TENT
Hire your ice skates at the door and enjoy this magnificent rink.
🗺 J22 ☎ 30 67 21 50 🚇 U- or S-Bahn Olympiazentrum

### RADIUS TOURISTIK
Rent a bike at the main rail station and explore the city with its 1,300km (800 miles) of cycle paths. The tourist office's city map for cyclists (on www.muenchen.de) will help you plan your route.
🗺 N22 ✉ Hauptbahnhof (near platform 33) ☎ 59 61 13 🚇 U- or S-Bahn Hauptbahnhof

### REITVEREIN CORONA
Get out of the city's hub and explore the Bavarian countryside on horseback.
🗺 Off map to south ✉ Muttenthalerstrasse 31 ☎ 79 80 80 🚇 S-Bahn Solln

### SPORTSCHECK
It takes an hour by car to the nearest ski slopes; this department store will organize your trip.
🗺 N23 ✉ Sendlinger Strasse 6 ☎ 21 66-0 🚇 U-Bahn Sendlinger Tor

## SPECTATOR SPORTS

### FOOTBALL
The atmosphere is electric when FC Bayern München or TSV 1860 play their home matches in the Olympic Stadium.
🗺 K22 ☎ 69 93 10 🚇 U-Bahn Olympiazentrum

### HORSE RACING
Flat racing is held weekly at the racecourse in Riem from March to November, while trotting races are held in nearby Daglfing.
🗺 Riem: off map to east; Daglfing: N29 ✉ Graf-Lehndorff-Strasse 36 ☎ Riem 9 45 52 30; Daglfing 9 30 00 10 🚇 S-Bahn Riem; S-Bahn Daglfing

### FOOTBALL FEVER
It is hardly surprising that football is Bavaria's most popular sport. FC Bayern München is at the top of the German league, with an international player in virtually every position. When the team is playing at home, massive crowds, decked from head to foot in red-and-white, throng the terraces of the Olympic Stadium, filling it to its capacity of 63,000. And this football fervour is likely to continue for a good while yet. In 2006, with the opening match of the World Cup scheduled to take place in Munich, everybody is eagerly awaiting the completion of a new stadium.

### ATTRACTIVE LANDSCAPES
The nearby towering Bavarian Alps and lakes remain popular destinations for Munich inhabitants seeking fresh air and recreation. On summer weekends many people escape the city to enjoy boating on the placid lakes or exhilarating walks in the picturesque countryside. In winter, skiers take to the road for the hour's journey to the snow-laden mountains.

# Where to Stay

## Luxury Hotels

### PRICES

Expect to pay the following per night for a double room:

Luxury      over €200

Mid-Range   €100–200

Budget      up to €100

### HOTEL SCENE

Like any metropolis, Munich can proudly claim a clutch of first-class hotels of worldwide reputation, but most of the city's 350 establishments are in the medium to lower price ranges. Except, that is, when a trade fair or the Oktoberfest (► 54) beer festival takes place, when prices can increase substantially. The Upper Bavarian countryside south of Munich is also well geared to welcoming tourists, thus offering the choice of staying in a nearby smaller town and commuting to the city by S-Bahn, train or bus.

### BAYERISCHER HOF
Classic, family-run hotel with excellent facilities including a roof-garden, health club, swimming pool and several top restaurants. 395 rooms.
✚ N23  ✉ Promenadeplatz 2–6  ☎ 2 12 00; www.bayerischehof.de  ◉ U- or S-Bahn Marienplatz

### EXCELSIOR
In the tranquil pedestrian zone, three minutes' walk from the main station. 113 rooms.
✚ N23  ✉ Schützenstrasse 11  ☎ 55 13 70; www.geisel-privatehotels.de  ◉ U- or S-Bahn Hauptbahnhof

### HILTON PARK
The Hilton has 479 rooms plus outdoor dining, beer garden, indoor pool, business centre, and views over the English Garden.
✚ M25  ✉ Am Tucherpark 7  ☎ 38 45-0; www.hilton.de  ◉ U-Bahn Giselastrasse  🚌 54

### KEMPINSKI HOTEL VIER JAHRESZEITEN
Munich's flagship hotel, perfectly placed on the city's most exclusive shopping street. It was established as a guest house for royalty visiting King Maximilian II and is still used today to accommodate visiting dignitaries. 316 rooms.
✚ N24  ✉ Maximilianstrasse 17  ☎ 21 25-0; www.kempinski-vierjahreszeiten.de  ◉ U-Bahn Odeonsplatz  🚌 Tram 19

### KÖNIGSHOF
One of Munich's top hotels with 87 rooms and one of the best restaurants in town.
✚ N23  ✉ Karlsplatz 25  ☎ 55 13 60; www.geisel-privatehotels.de  ◉ U- or S-Bahn Karlsplatz

### MANDARIN ORIENTAL
Guests at this 73-room, luxury hotel have included Prince Charles and Madonna.
✚ N24  ✉ Neuturmstrasse 1  ☎ 29 09 80; www.mandarinoriental.com  ◉ U- or S-Bahn Marienplatz

### OPERA
A small homely hotel, with 25 rooms, set in a delightful old mansion with an inner courtyard.
✚ N24  ✉ St.-Anna-Strasse 10  ☎ 210 49 40; www.hotel-opera.de  ◉ U-Bahn Lehel

### PLATZL
A friendly hotel with 167 traditional rooms. Top-class facilities include a fitness area and a beautiful restaurant in a converted mill.
✚ N24  ✉ Sparkassenstrasse 10  ☎ 23 70 30; www.platzl.de  ◉ U- or S-Bahn Marienplatz

### PRINZREGENT
Tradition and comfort combine at this elegant hotel, with 65 rooms and an attractive garden.
✚ N25  ✉ Ismaningerstrasse 42-44  ☎ 41 60 50; www.prinzregent.de  ◉ U-Bahn Max-Weber-Platz

### RITZI
The aptly-named Ritzi is central yet quiet, with 25 stylish rooms. It has a trendy bar and serves a great buffet breakfast.
✚ M25  ✉ Maria-Theresiastrasse 2a  ☎ 4 19 50 30; www.hotelritzi.de  ◉ U-Bahn Max-Weber-Platz

## Where to Stay

# Mid-Range Hotels

**ADMIRAL**
This smart Hotel Garni with 33 rooms, near the river, offers special weekend packages.
🏠 O24 ✉ Kohlstrasse 9 ☎ 21 63 50; www.hotel-admiral.de 🚇 S-Bahn Isartor

**ANNA**
A tasteful, modern hotel with 56 rooms, near to the main railway station, with underground parking facilities and young, helpful staff.
🏠 N23 ✉ Schützenstrasse 1 ☎ 59 99 40; www.geisel-privatehotels.de 🚇 U- or S-Bahn Hauptbahnhof

**CARLTON**
A hidden treasure for those in the know, this 49-room hotel, close to Odeonsplatzis, is reasonably priced.
🏠 M24 ✉ Fürstenstrasse 12 ☎ 28 20 61; www.renner-hotel.og.de 🚇 U-Bahn Odeonsplatz

**CORTIINA**
Smart, minimalist hotel frequented by a super-chic clientele. Internet portal in all 35 rooms.
🏠 N24 ✉ Ledererstrasse 8 ☎ 2 42 24 90; www.cortiina.com 🚇 U- or S-Bahn Marienplatz

**COSMOPOLITAN**
Simple, modern, hotel with 71 rooms. Surprisingly quiet considering it is in the heart of Schwabing.
🏠 L24 ✉ Hohenzollernstrasse 5 ☎ 3 83 81-0; www.geisel-privatehotels.de 🚇 U-Bahn Giselastrasse, Münchener Freiheit 🚌 33

**EXQUISIT**
A small, elegant hotel with a choice of 50 rooms, in a secluded side street near the site where the Oktoberfest takes place.
🏠 N23 ✉ Pettenkoferstrasse 3 ☎ 5 51 99 00; www.hotel-exquisit.com 🚇 U-Bahn Sendlinger Tor

**GÄSTEHAUS ENGLISCHER GARTEN**
An oasis on the edge of the English Garden; only 12 rooms in the main building and 13 in the annexe. Reserve well ahead.
🏠 L25 ✉ Liebergesellstrasse 8 ☎ 3 83 94 10; www.hotel englischergarten.de 🚇 U-Bahn Münchener Freiheit

**INSELMÜHLE**
This beautifully renovated, timbered corn mill is one of the 'Romantik' chain of hotels and has 38 rooms. Just outside the city but worth the extra trip.
🏠 J17 ✉ Von-Kahr-Strasse 87 ☎ 8 10 10; www.weber-gastronomie.de 🚇 S-Bahn Allach

**PARK PLAZA**
In the Schwabing area, this modern, 156-room hotel makes a good base for sightseeing and dining out.
🏠 L24 ✉ Leopoldstrasse 132 ☎ 3 61 95 70; www.parkplaza europe.com 🚇 U-Bahn Dietlindenstrasse

**SPLENDID-DOLLMANN**
A small, exclusive hotel in central Munich, with 37 rooms decorated in a range of styles including baroque, Louis XIV and Bavarian.
🏠 N24 ✉ Thierschstrasse 49 ☎ 29 66 06; www.hotel-splendid-dollmann.de 🚇 U-Bahn Lehel

### BOOKINGS

Wherever you see the following signs: *Hotel, Pension, Gasthof, Gasthaus, Gaststätte, Gästehaus, Fremdenzimmer* and *Ferienwohnungen*, you will find accommodation. Reserve as early as possible to avoid disappointment. Prices quoted always include service and taxes, and usually breakfast.

## Where to Stay

# Budget Accomodation

### CAMPING

For really cheap accommodation in Munich, why not bring a tent? There are three campsites in and around Munich. The best, and the most central, is Camping Thalkirchen (☎ 723 17 07; www.camping.muenchen.de), attractively positioned along the River Isar, with 700 places open from mid-March until the end of October. There is no need to reserve except during the Oktoberfest.

### AM MARKT

A traditional hotel with 32 rooms, on one of the last original old squares near the Viktualienmarket.
✚ N24 ✉ Heiliggeiststrasse 6 ☎ 22 50 14 Ⓢ U- or S-Bahn Marienplatz

### BED AND BREAKFAST

This company organizes rooms in private homes and apartments in the city and on the outskirts.
✚ M21 ✉ Schulstrasse 36 ☎ 1 68 87 81 Ⓢ U-Bahn Rotkreuzplatz

### BELLE BLUE

This modern, minimalist pension is located near the main railway station and has 30 rooms.
✚ N23 ✉ Schillerstrasse 21 ☎ 5 50 62 60; www.hotel-belleblue.com Ⓢ U- or S-Bahn Hauptbahnhof

### BLAUER BOCK

A central hotel with 75 cosy rooms and parking facilities. Great value.
✚ N23 ✉ Sebastiansplatz 9 ☎ 23 17 80; www.blauerbock-muenchen.de Ⓢ U- or S-Bahn Marienplatz

### BURG SCHWANECK

A long way from the heart of the city, this youth hostel is housed in a castle overlooking the River Isar. Youth hostel pass required.
✚ Off map to south ✉ Burgweg 4–6, Pullach ☎ 74 48 66 70; www.burgschwaneck.de Ⓢ S-Bahn Pullach

### HAUS INTERNATIONAL

Slightly more expensive than youth hostels but you don't have to belong to a youth hostel organization to stay here.
✚ L23 ✉ Elisabethstrasse 87 ☎ 12 00 60; www.haus-international.de Ⓢ U-Bahn Hohenzollernplatz

### JUGENDHERBERGE MÜNCHEN (MUNICH YOUTH HOSTEL)

Advance reservations and a youth hostel pass are essential here.
✚ M21 ✉ Wendl-Dietrich-Strasse 20 ☎ 13 11 56; www.muenchen-nenhausen.jugendherberge.de Ⓢ U-Bahn Rotkreuzplatz

### MITWOHNBÖRSE– HOME COMPANY

Useful for longer stays, the Mitwohnzentrale will arrange apartment accommodation in Munich for a small fee.
✚ L23 ✉ Germaniastrasse 20 ☎ 1 94 45; www.muenchen.homecompany.de Ⓢ U-Bahn Dietlindenstrasse

### PENSION FRANK

Models in town for photo calls often stay in this popular hotel, with 19 reasonably priced rooms, in the heart of trendy Schwabing.
✚ M24 ✉ Schellingstrasse 24 ☎ 28 14 51; www.pension-frank.de Ⓢ U-Bahn Universität

### STEFANIE

A clean, friendly pension with 32 rooms in the popular university district a short distance from the three Pinakothek galleries.
✚ M24 ✉ Türkenstrasse 35 ☎ 2 88 14 00; www.hotel-stefanie.de Ⓢ U-Bahn Universität

# MUNICH
## travel facts

Essential Facts  *90*

Getting Around  *90–91*

Media & Communications  *92*

Emergencies  *92*

Tourist Offices  *93*

Language  *93*

Travel facts

## ESSENTIAL FACTS

### Customs regulations
- Duty-free limits for non-European Union visitors are: 200 cigarettes or 250g of tobacco or 50 cigars; 2 litres of wine and 1 litre of spirits.

### Electricity
- 220 volts; two-pin sockets. Take an adaptor with you.

### Etiquette
- Say *Grüss Gott* (good day) and *Auf Wiedersehen* (goodbye) when shopping, *Guten Appetit* (enjoy your meal) when eating, *Entschuldigen Sie* (excuse me) in crowds.
- Never jump lights at pedestrian crossings. Don't walk on cycle paths.
- Dress is generally informal, except for the theatre, opera or nightclubs.
- Service is officially included in bills but tipping is customary.

### Lavatories
- *Toiletten* are marked *Herren* (men) and *Damen* (women). *Besetzt* means occupied, *frei* means vacant. There is often a small charge.

### National holidays
- 1 January, 6 January, Good Friday, Easter Sunday, Easter Monday, 1 May, Ascension Day, Whit Sunday and Whit Monday, Corpus Christi, 15 August, 3 October, 1 November, 3rd/4th week in November: Day of Repentance and Prayer, Christmas Day, 26 December.

### Opening hours
- Banks: Mon–Fri 8.30–3.45 (some open Thu to 5.30, many close for lunch).
- Shops: Mon–Fri 9–6, may change to 9–8 (late shopping Thu until 8.30), Sat 9–2, (but to 4 or 6pm on first Sat in the month). Many close for lunch (noon–2).
- Museums and galleries: Tue–Sun 9 or 10am–5. Most close Mon and public holidays. Many free on Sun.

### Places of worship
- Roman Catholic: Frauenkirche, Peterskirche, and many others.
- Roman Catholic Services in English: at 10.30am in Kaulbachstrasse 33 and at 6pm in Kreuzkirche, Kreuzstrasse 2.
- Contact the tourist office (➤ 93) for details of the following:
- Jewish: ✉ Reichenbachstrasse 27
- Muslim: Mosque ✉ Wallnerstrasse 1–3
- English services: International Baptist Church ✉ Holzstrasse 9; Evangelical International Community Church ✉ Enhuberstrasse 10

### Student travellers
- Some museums and theatres offer up to 50 per cent discounts with an International Student ID Card.
- A German Rail Youth Pass is available for young people under 26, valid for 5, 10 or 15 days. Must be purchased outside Germany.
- For budget accommodation, camping and youth hostels (➤ 88).

### Women travellers
- Frauenhaus München offers 24-hour help for women ☎ 35 48 30
- Some car parks have well-lit, reserved parking for women only near the main entrance 🅿 025 ✉ Gasteig, Rosenheimerstrasse 5 🕐 6.30am–midnight; 🅿 N23 ✉ Conti-Parkhaus am Stachus Sonnen-Heizoqspitalstrasse 🕐 24 hours

## GETTING AROUND

- Munich has an excellent, albeit complicated, public transport network, with two urban railways (S-Bahn rapid transit and U-Bahn

subway), and a comprehensive network of bus and tram routes.
- The local transport authority is the Münchner Verkehrs- und Tarifverbund (MVV) ✚ N24 ✉ Thierschstrasse 2 ☎ 41 42 43 44

## Types of ticket
- The MVV network is divided into fare zones. Prices are based on the number of zones required to complete the trip. For most sightseeing you will remain in the *Innenraum* (interior area—marked blue on station maps). To travel further you need a ticket valid for the *Gesamtnetz* (total network).
- Travelling without a valid ticket can result in a heavy fine.
- *Kurzstrecken*: short trip single tickets can be bought for journeys covering only four stops; two may be U- or S-Bahn stops. A trip must not last more than one hour and can only be used in one direction. Unlimited transfers are permitted.
- *Streifenkarte*: a strip of tickets. For each journey, stamp the appropriate number of strips. A 'short trip' is one strip. More than two U- or S-Bahn stops within one zone is two strips. If you are travelling outside the blue *Innenraum* zone, a notice shows how many strips you need to punch.
- *Einzelfahrkarte*: single tickets can be bought covering any number of zones, but a *Streifenkarte* usually works out cheaper.
- *Tageskarte*: one day's unlimited travel from 9am until 6am the following day. Purchase either a *Single-Tageskarte* for one person, or a *Partner-Tageskarte* for up to five people (maximum two adults).
- *Isacard*: a weekly ticket providing unlimited travel on MVV transport, available at MVV ticket offices or ticket vending machines.

## Discounts
- Children under six travel free and aged six to 14 at reduced fares.
- The Munich Welcome card, available from tourist offices, the main train station and some hotels, provides unlimited travel for 24 hours on all public transport plus savings of up to 50 per cent on admission to major city attractions including museums, city tours, bicycle rentals and the zoo. It is also available as a three-day ticket or a three-day partner ticket.

## The U- and S-Bahn
- Smoking is banned on trains and in the stations.
- Bicycles may be taken on the trains all day Sat, Sun and public holidays; on weekdays not at rush hour (6–9am, 4–6pm).

## Trams
- Scenic routes: trams 18, 19, 20, 21 and 27 operate around the old town; tram 20 goes to the English Garden; tram 27 is useful for exploring Schwabing.

## Maps and timetables
- MVV station ticket offices and tourist information centres supply free maps and information.

## Taxis
- Taxis are cream-coloured; stands are throughout the city.
- Not particularly cheap; small surcharge for luggage.
- Car hire: Avis ☎ (01805) 557755
- Central taxi stand ☎ 2 16 10
- Chauffeur service Sixt ☎ (01805) 002210
- For more information on getting around ➤ 7.

## Travel facts

### MEDIA & COMMUNICATIONS

#### Newspapers and magazines
- Bavaria's daily paper, *Süddeutsche Zeitung*, is published in Munich.
- Munich has several local dailies—*Münchner Abendzeitung*, *tz* and *Bild-Zeitung*.
- An English-language listings magazine, *Munich Found*, is available from major newsagents.

#### Post offices
- Main post office is opposite the railway station ✉ Bahnhofplatz 1 ☎ 5 99 08 70 🕒 Mon– Fri 7am–8pm, Sat 9–4
- Most other post offices are open Mon–Fri 8am–noon, 3–6pm, Sat 8am–noon.
- Post boxes are bright yellow and clearly marked 'Munich' and 'other places' (*Andere Orte*).
- All letters to the UK and EU countries cost €.055. The cost for airmail letters to the US and Canada is €1.55 for the first 5 grams, and €1 for postcards.

#### Telephones
- Coin/phonecard telephones are cheaper than hotel telephones. Purchase phonecards at post offices and newsagents.
- Make long-distance calls from boxes marked International or from telephones in post offices.
- Cheap rate: between 6pm and 8am on weekdays; all day at weekends.
- National enquiries ☎ 011 88.
- International enquiries ☎ 00 118.
- To call Munich from abroad, dial 00, followed by Germany's country code 49, then the area code 89, followed by the number.
- To phone home from Munich, dial 00 followed by your own country code (UK 44, Ireland 353, US and Canada 1, Australia 61, New Zealand 64), then the number.

### EMERGENCIES

#### Embassies/consulates
- UK ✉ Bürkleinstrasse 10 ☎ 21 10 90
- US ✉ Königinstrasse 5 ☎ 2 88 80
- Canada ✉ Tal 29 ☎ 2 19 95 70

#### Emergency phone numbers
- Police ☎ 110
- Fire ☎ 112
- Ambulance ☎ 110 and 112 and 192 22
- Medical emergency service ☎ 192 22
- Dental emergency service ☎ 723 30-93/94
- Poisons emergency service ☎ 192 40
- Rape hotline ☎ 76 37 37
- Breakdown service ☎ (01802) 222222

#### Lost property
- Municipal lost property office: ✉ Oetztalerstrasse 17 🕒 Mon–Thu 8–noon, (also Tue 2–6.30), Fri 7–noon ☎ 2 33 00
- For anything lost on the urban rail, underground, tram or bus contact MVV (☎ 41 42 43 44) for the individual transport company number.
- For items left on Deutsche Bahn trains: Fundbüro der Bundesbahn ✉ Hauptbahnhof, opposite platform 26 🕒 Mon–Fri 6.30am–11.30pm, Sat 7.30am–10.45pm, Sun 7.30am–11pm ☎ 13 08 66-64

#### Medical treatment
- A list of English-speaking doctors is available at the British and US Consulates.

#### Medicines and pharmacies
- Pack enough of any prescription medication you take regularly to last for the duration of your trip.
- Every neighbourhood has a 24-hour pharmacy (*Apotheke*). Look for the address of that night's 24-hour *Apotheke* displayed

## Travel facts

in the window.
- International pharmacies have staff who speak different languages. Try Bahnhof-Apotheke ✚ N22 ✉ Bahnhofplatz 2 ☎ 59 41 19 or Internationale Ludwigs-Apotheke ✚ N23 ✉ Neuhauserstrasse 11 ☎ 18 94 01 00

### Sensible precautions
- Munich is one of the safer European cities, but tourists should remain on their guard.
- At night, avoid poorly lit areas and the seedy red-light district behind the main railway station.

## TOURIST OFFICES

- Hauptbahnhof ☎ 23 39 65 00 🕒 Mon–Sat 9–8, Sun 10–6
- Neues Rathaus ✉ Marienplatz 🕒 Mon–Fri 10–8, Sat 10–4

### German National Tourist Offices
- UK ✉ PO Box 2695, London W1A 3TN ☎ 020 7317 0908
- US ✉ 122 East 42nd Street, New York, NY 10168–0072 ☎ (212) 661 7200

## LANGUAGE

**no** nein
**please** bitte
**thank you** danke
**hello** Grüss Gott
**good morning** guten Morgen
**good evening** guten Abend
**good night** gute Nacht
**goodbye** auf Wiedersehen
**excuse me please** entschuldigen Sie bitte
**do you speak English?** sprechen Sie Englisch?
**I don't understand** ich verstehe nicht
**today** heute
**yesterday** gestern
**tomorrow** morgen

**small/large** klein/gross
**cold/hot** kalt/warm
**good** gut
**menu** die Speisekarte
**breakfast** das Frühstück
**lunch** das Mittagesen
**dinner** das Abendessen
**white wine** der Weisswein
**red wine** der Rotwein
**beer** das Bier
**bread** das Brot
**milk** die Milch
**sugar** der Zucker
**water** das Wasser
**bill (check)** die Rechnung
**room** das Zimmer
**right/left** rechts/links
**straight on** geradeaus
**near/far** nahe/weit
**open** offen
**closed** geschlossen
**how much does it cost?** wieviel kostet es?
**expensive** teuer
**inexpensive** billig
**Where are the lavatories?** Wo sind die Toiletten?
**Where's the bank?** Wo ist die Bank?
**station** der Bahnhof
**airport** der Flughafen
**post office** das Postamt
**chemist** die Apotheke
**police** die Polizei
**hospital** das Krankenhaus
**doctor** der Arzt

1 eins
2 zwei
3 drei
4 vier
5 fünf
6 sechs
7 sieben
8 acht
9 neun
10 zehn
11 elf
12 zwölf
20 zwanzig

# Index

## A
accommodation 86–88
Ahnengalerie 45
airport 6
Alte Pinakothek 33
Altes Rathaus 42
Amazeum 62
Ammersee 55
Ancestral Portrait Gallery 45
Angel of Peace 60
Antiquarium 44
Archbishop's Palace 22
Asam-Schlössl 'Maria Einsiedel' 58
Asamkirche 37
Auer Mai Dult 4
Augustiner Keller 52
Aumeister 52

## B
Bad Tölz 21
Badenburg 26
ballet 82, 83
banks 90
Bavarian Film Studios 62
Bavarian National Museum 30, 50
Bavarian restaurants 65
Bavarian State Art Collection 30
Bavarian State Chancellery 61
Bavarian State Gallery of Modern Art 56
Bavarian State Opera 47, 83
Bayerische Staatsoper 47
Bayerisches National-museum 30, 50
beer halls and beer gardens 46, 52–53
Blombergbahn 21
BMW Headquarters 61
BMW-Museum 28
bookshops 72, 77
Bräustüberl Weihenstephan 52
breakfast cafés 69
Brunnenbuberl 60
buses, long-distance 6

## C
cafés 68–70, 80, 81
camping 88
Carmelite Church 22
castles 58, 59
Chiemsee 21
children's entertainment 62, 82–83
Chinese Tower 49
Chinesischer Turm 49
Christkindlmarkt 54
Christmas Market 54
churches 58, 59, 90
cinemas 79
Circus Krone 62
City Gallery in the Lenbachhaus 31
climate 4
Coin Museum 45
Court Garden 44
crown jewels 45
currency 6
customs regulations 90
Cuvilliés Theatre 45
cybercafés 5

## D
Dachau 29, 59
Dachau Concentration Camp Memorial 29
Damenstiftskirche St. Anna 58
Deutsches Museum 48
Devil's Footprint 39
Diessen 55
discount travel tickets 91
districts 10
Dreifaltigkeitskirche 58
driving 7

## E
eating out 64–71
Egyptian Art Museum 45
electricity 90
embassies and consulates 92–93
emergencies 92
Englischer Garten 49
English Garden 49
entertainment 79–85
entry requirements 6
Erwin von Kreibig Gallery 56
etiquette 90
excursions 20–21

## F
Fairground Museum 38
Fasching 54
Feldherrnhalle 44
Feldmochingersee 55
Feringasee 55
festivals and events 4, 54
Flaucher, Zum 53
Flugwerft Schleissheim 56
fountains 60
Frauenkirche 39

## G
Gasteig 83
German Art and Antiques Fair 4
German Hunting and Fishing Museum 56
German Theatre Museum 56
Glockenspiel 40
Glyptothek 32

## H
Hackerkeller 52
Hall of Mirrors 26
Haus der Kunst 56
Heiliggeistkirche 58
Hellabrunn Zoo 62
Herrenchiemsee 21
Hirschgarten 52–53
history 16–17
History of Munich Museum 38
Hofbräuhaus 46
Hofgarten 44
Holy Ghost, Church of the 58
Holy Trinity, Church of the 58
Hypobank 61

## I
insurance 7
International Youth Library 59

## J
Jacobi Dult 4
Japanese Tea House 49
Japanisches Teehaus 49
Jugendstilhaus Ainmillerstrasse 61

## K
Karlsfelder See 55
Kleinhesseloher See 49
Kloster Andechs 55
Königsplatz 32
Kulturzentrum Gasteig 61

94

## Index

### L
lakes 55
language 93
lavatories 90
Lenbachhaus 13
Leuchtenberg-Palais 44
lost property 92
Löwenbräukeller 53
Ludwigskirche 59

### M
Magdalenenklause 26
Mann, Thomas 13
maps and timetables 91
Mariensäule 60
Marionette Theatre Collection 38
markets 43, 74, 75
Marstallmuseum 26
Max-Emanuel-Brauerei 53
medical treatment 92
Meissen Porcelain Museum 30
Menterschwaige 53
Michaelskirche 36
Military Commanders' Hall 44
money 6
Monopteros 49
Munich City Museum 38
Munich nightlife 24
Munich Welcome card 91
Museum Mensch und Natur 62
Museum Villa Stuck 57
museums and galleries 56–57, 90
music 80–83
Musikhochschule 61
MVV transport network 7, 91

### N
national holidays 90
national identity cards 6
Nationaltheater 47, 83
Neue Pinakothek 34
Neuschwanstein 20
Neues Rathaus 40
New Palace 30
New Picture Gallery 34
newspapers and magazines 92
nightclubs 79
nightlife 24

### O
Odeonsplatz 44
*Oktoberfest* 54
Old Palace 30
Old Picture Gallery 33
Old Town 22
Old Town Hall 42
Olympiapark 27
opening hours 90
opera 47, 82, 83

### P
Palace Lustheim 30
Palazzo Branca 34
passports 6
Peterskirche 41
personal safety 93
pharmacies 92–93
Photography and Film Museum 38
Pinakothek der Moderne 35
places of worship 90
Planetarium 48
police 92
Porcelain Museum 26
post offices 92
Post-und-Wohngebäude 61
Propyläen 32
public transport 7, 90–91

### R
rail services 7
Residenz 45
Rosengarten im Westpark 53

### S
St. Emmeramsmühle 53
St. John Nepomuk, Church of 37
St. Michael, Church of 36
Schack-Galerie 57
Schatzkammer 45
Schleissheim Palaces 30
Schloss Blutenburg 58, 59
Schloss Dachau 59
Schloss Fürstenried 59
Schloss Nymphenburg 26
Schloss Suresnes 59
Sculpture Museum 32
shopping 18–19, 72–78

sightseeing, organized 20
specialist shops 19, 76–77
Spielzeugmuseum 42

sport 84–85
Staatliche Antikensammlung 32
Staatsgalerie Moderner Kunst 56
Staatskanzlei 61
Städtische Galerie im Lenbachhaus 31
Stadtmuseum 38
Starkbierzeit 54
Starnberger See 55
State Collection of Antiquities 32
Steiff teddy bears 42, 77
Strauss, Richard 17
student travellers 90

### T
taxis 7, 91
Taxisgarten 53
telephones 92
Theatinerkirche 44, 59
theatre 82–83
time differences 4
tourist offices 93
Toy Museum 42
trains 7, 91
trams 7, 91
travelling in Munich 6–7, 90–91
Treasury 45

### U
U-Bahn and S-Bahn 7, 90, 91
Utting 55

### V
Valentin-Museum 57
Viktualienmarkt 43
visitors with disabilities 7
visas 6

### W
Waldwirtschaft Grosshesselohe 53
Walking Man 60
walks 22–23, 24
websites 9
women travellers 90

### Z
ZAM (Centre for Extraordinary Museums)

95

# Citypack
## munich's 25 best

**AUTHOR AND EDITION REVISER** Teresa Fisher
**MANAGING EDITORS** Apostrophe S Limited
**COVER DESIGN** Tigist Getachew, Fabrizio La Rocca

Copyright © Automobile Association Developments Limited 1997, 2001, 2004, 2005

All rights reserved under International and Pan-American Copyright Conventions. Published in the United States by Fodor's Travel, a division of Random House, Inc., and simultaneously in Canada by Random House of Canada Limited, Toronto. Distributed by Random House, Inc., New York. No maps, illustrations, or other portions of this book may be reproduced in any form without written permission from the publishers.

Fodor's is a registered trademark of Random House, Inc.
Published in the United Kingdom by AA Publishing

**ISBN 13: 978-1-4000-1582-5**
**ISBN 10: 1-4000-1582-0**

**THIRD EDITION**

**ACKNOWLEDGMENTS**
The author wishes to thank Deutsche B.A., the Hotel Angleterre, the Munich Tourist Office, Christian and Annelies Hess, Michaela Netzer and Emmanuel Vermot for their help.
The Automobile Association would like to thank the following photographers, libraries and agencies for their assistance in the preparation of this book.
Illustrated London News 17; Bridgeman Art Library, London 34c *The Laundress* by Edgar Degas; Teresa Fisher 32; ©Bayerische Staatsgenälde/Haydar Kajupinar 57; Pinakothek der Moderne 35; Edmund Nagele FRPS 27t; Stockbyte 5; Toy Museum 42t, 62
The remaining images are held in the Association's own library (AA WORLD TRAVEL LIBRARY) and were taken by A Souter; with the exception of 9ct, 18/19, 21c, 55 which were taken by Adrian Baker; 22c which was taken by Peter Davison; and 8bl, 8r, 10c, 11t, 11b, 17r, 23, 24cl, 24cr, 25, 26c, 31c, 33b, 34t, 36t, 39t, 39c, 40, 42c, 43t, 43c, 46r, 48t, 50t, 50c, 51t, 51b, 53, 60, 61, 63b, 87t which were taken by Clive Sawyer.

**IMPORTANT TIP**
Time inevitably brings changes, so always confirm prices, travel facts, and other perishable information when it matters. Although Fodor's cannot accept responsibility for errors, you can use this guide in the confidence that we have taken every care to ensure its accuracy.

**SPECIAL SALES**
This book is available for special discounts for bulk purchases for sales promotions or premiums. Special editions, including personalized covers, excerpts of existing guides, and corporate imprints, can be created in large quantities for special needs. For more information, write to Special Marketing/Premium Sales, 1745 Broadway, MD 6–2, New York, NY 10019 or email specialmarkets@randomhouse.com.

Colour separation by Keenes, Andover
Manufactured by Hang Tai D&P Limited, Hong Kong
10 9 8 7 6 5 4 3 2

A03204
Fold out map © MAIRDUMONT / Falk Verlag 2006
Transport map © Communicarta Ltd, UK

**DESTINATIONS COVERED BY THE CITYPACK SERIES**
• Amsterdam • Bangkok • Barcelona • Beijing • Berlin • Boston • Brussels & Bruges •
• Chicago • Dublin • Florence • Hong Kong • Lisbon • Ljubljana • London • Los Angeles •
• Madrid • Melbourne • Miami • Milan • Montréal • Munich • Naples • New York • Paris •
• Prague • Rome • San Francisco • Seattle • Shanghai • Singapore • Sydney • Tokyo •
• Toronto • Venice • Vienna • Washington DC •